The Ugly Man Sits
in the Garden

Pieces of a Life

Andy Weinberger

Andy Wein...

Bread &
Butter
Books

*For Linda ~
These are Pieces of
my life. I hope they
become yours as well.
with thanks,
Andy*

Published 2016 by Bread & Butter Books
Sonoma, California

ISBN 978-0-692-75256-2

The essays in this book were previously published on the Readers' Books website, www.readersbooks.com, betweeen 2003 and 2016.

Book and cover design by Leslie V. Carlson Information Design
Cover illustration by Chester Arnold
Photo of the author by Lilla G. Weinberger
Typeset in Chaparral Pro

Printed by Sumi Printing

Contents

Introduction

The following pieces are not in any particular order. They are arranged, or disarranged, or deranged—depending on your point of view—for your enjoyment, pure and simple. It turns out that I've been writing these things for years and while there are, to date, some four hundred pieces, we've decided to spare you, and we've culled it down to the one hundred best. I say "best" advisedly, because although many of them are glib and facile (one might even say slick), I am not under the illusion that I come within a mile of the razor-sharp intellects of Isaiah Berlin or E.B. White. No, this is just what spilled out of me on a given day. Think of it as verbal sweat, or, if you don't care for sweat, some other form of verbal residue.

Many of these essays deal with the bookstore, my life as a bookseller in Sonoma, and how the love and reading of books places us in the larger firmament. Some talk about our customers; why they are so important to us; how the bookstore sustains them; and how they have reciprocated over time. I think in general, one could apply the same standard to any retail business in any small town. Having said that, it's also true that a bookstore is not just any retail business. Choosing and buying a book is a personal experience, unlike, say choosing and buying deodorant or a pair of socks or a hammer. When you buy a book to read, you're welcoming those words, those characters, that story, into your mind. You have to make room for it among all your other cherished ideas; it may haunt your dreams; it may change your life forever. You can't say the same thing about a hammer.

A few pieces touch on politics or current events, although I believe most of those have been deleted because of their ephemeralness. I mean, does anyone even think about Mitt Romney anymore? Or Sarah Palin's views on foreign policy? Please.

If I had to choose, I'd say the best ones of this lot concern my family, their idiosyncrasies, and the lessons I somehow learned growing up and watching them live their lives. In particular, I need to acknowledge what a huge influence my father has been on my overall development. Readers' Books would not be here today without his support and encouragement. And though we often disagreed on many things, the older I get, the more I seem to be strolling down the same pathways he did, and possibly even having the same thoughts. He and my mom would have enjoyed these little vignettes, I'm pretty sure. Of course, since they're both long gone, there's no way to test this theory. But even if they hated these pieces, I know they would both be smart enough to keep their mouths shut. For their silent approval, therefore, they have my eternal thanks. This book is for them.

Some Things Just Can't Be Explained
May 31, 2014

This week, were she still alive, my mother would be turning one hundred years old. Even more than life, I credit her with giving me a deep love of music and language. She was the one who sat me down at the piano at the age of—oh, I couldn't have been more than three or four—and delighted in whatever mish-mash I hammered out. She was never happier than when she was scribbling little poems for special occasions ("Happy birthday, darling boy/You are both our pride and joy/Don't reply/You needn't bother/Love, Your Mother and your Father"). Maybe I caught the writing bug from her. She was the one who praised my early writing, after all. And although she was the first one in her family to graduate from high school, she never went any further, never took the necessary prerequisite courses to obtain a college degree. She was a dabbler, I guess you'd say, or what we might today call a "lifelong learner." Although forever enrolled at Pasadena City College, she was always taking the introductory course in whatever foreign language she was smitten with at the time. She would usually get an A, and if she loved the teacher, which was often the case, she would sign up again for the same introductory class.

Apart from being the teacher's pet, though, I reckoned that my mom's passion for foreign languages had more to do with entertainment than with actually saying anything meaningful. If she met a man or woman from France or Mexico or Japan, she would automatically burst out with some little "how are you" phrase that would cause them to smile and marvel politely, but of course, the conversation could never go too far beyond that. It didn't matter really; it was just her way of touching base and welcoming them into her cosmopolitan, junior college realm. Not that it always worked with every language. I remember her saying that the hardest course she ever took was Arabic, from which she only could retain one exasperating sentence: The ugly man sits in the garden.

Scientists say there is a link in the brain between music and language and math, i.e., those who are talented musicians tend to be facile foreign language speakers and good at math. Maybe if you think of math as another language this makes more sense, although I doubt that even Einstein himself would ever be able to numerically express something as obtuse as the ugly man sits in the garden. But my mom could. In Arabic, no less.

Enter (and Exit) Laughing
May 2012

Yesterday my dear friend, Maureen, came into the store, took one look at me and said: "You are soooo funny! Those email essays of yours, I just look forward to them every Saturday after lunch. You know what they do? They make me laugh out loud. Well, not all of them. But most of them. And the world needs laughter, God knows. Has anyone ever told you how funny they are? Have you ever thought of bundling them up and publishing them in a book? Why don't you? I'd buy a book like that, I would, I would."

You really think they're funny? I thought to myself. I think they're kind of sad, actually. Okay, the stuff about my parents and aunts and uncles may be funny, but that's because my family has always had funny tattooed into their DNA, it's how they survived when the wolf was at the door—by telling jokes. This isn't unusual, in my opinion. Anyone who grew up not belonging, anyone who was raised, say, Russian-Hungarian-Jewish-Gypsy-Socialist (a natural-born son of the Marx Brothers, in other words) has had all kinds of bizarre experiences: there's no way around it. And bizarre can be funny. It depends on your delivery.

Somebody was asking me about Easter last month, how we celebrated it. He didn't know I was Jewish. I said, "Well, to tell you the truth, we don't do much anymore, but back in the olden days, in Kiev, we used to celebrate Easter by hiding under the floorboards."

He didn't get it.

I've told a lot of jokes, and let me tell you, there's nothing worse than somebody who just looks at you blankly after a punch line and says, huh? I mean, it's like you've been talking to a mattress; your whole reason for being has been called into question. When a joke falls flat like that you are suddenly an orphan—all alone in the universe.

Towards the end of his life, my dad became an ardent connoisseur of jokes. He would collect them meticulously, memorize them (not an easy job at 85 years old), and try them out on me. And when someone told me one, I would always make sure to pass it on to him. Some of these jokes were off-color; some were partly in Yiddish; some were shaggy dog stories; and a few, I have to say, were politically incorrect. It didn't matter. We had a currency, my father and I, we both spoke the language of humor, and, while it lasted, we poked fun at everything, and it was wonderful. Thinking back, those jokes and the laughter we exchanged did more to give me an appreciation of his life than all the journals and photo albums that he left behind.

But I don't know if Maureen's right about a book of emails. I mean, life is short enough as it is. Really, she should be satisfied just smiling now and then. And of course I think it's very good if somehow I make her laugh out loud; in fact, it probably helps her digestion.

Adios, Reva
July 20, 2013

We all knew this was coming, that there would be an announcement, simple and to the point: our dear friend, loyal customer, and devoted booster, Reva Metzger, has died at last. She'd been ill for a while, and there was no good prognosis, no light at the end of the tunnel. All we could do was wait and hope that when it happened, she would die peacefully and without pain. I wish I could say I was relieved to hear that she slipped away from us in just such a fashion—no muss, no fuss—that her death was "easy" as those things go. But there's a selfish part of me that yearns for her to stick around.

Reva was a fighter for lost causes, a do-gooder in the best sense of that word, a woman who, although she herself was the most disorganized person on the planet, still managed to pull together individuals from all over town and cajole them into getting the job done. It was Reva who came to us in the depths of the last recession and said, I don't want Readers' Books to disappear. What can I do to help? It was Reva and her army of friends who launched the big fund-raising drive that built the Reading Garden that graces our store today with its spectacular flower bed and fountain, Reva who fronted the money and got the ball rolling. The Reading Garden is—besides the books and our staff—one of the crown jewels of this place. We've used it for book talks, poetry and play readings, jazz concerts, and, of course, Random Acts, our monthly venture into the unknown land of the open mic.

What I'm trying to say is that we owe a lot to Reva Metzger, that just one caring and determined visionary can make an enormous difference in the lives of us all. We get lots of praise from our customers for what a great store we have, that this is always the first place they stop when they come to town, that Sonoma wouldn't be the same, etc. I appreciate those sentiments, I do. But what really makes this town special is the people who live here, the givers—the quiet, steadfast, unsung heroes like Reva.

Reva Metzger had the purest of hearts. In fact, she was all heart.

Looking Back
September 24, 2011

A couple of weeks ago, Random Acts held their monthly shindig in our Reading Garden. It coincided (more or less) with the 10th anniversary of the tragic events of 9/11, and so some folks brought forth their memories of that dark time in poetry and prose. I read a poem by Jane Hirshfield, and sang a couple of sentimental tunes my parents used to sing. For me, September 11th is all about my father, and here's why: My dad was a news junkie. He watched CNN religiously, morning, noon, and night. When the World Trade Center was hit, he camped out in the living room to watch, and over the course of the next month he must have seen the footage of those planes slamming into those buildings a thousand times. Not long after that, he was diagnosed with cancer. I don't know what the medical world would say about whether that kind of intense television viewing is toxic or not. What I do know is that he died on September 10th, 2002, and the next day, September 11th, we buried him in Santa Rosa. One year to the day. I think of him now as "collateral damage"—another victim of that experience. He wasn't at Ground Zero, but for my money, he might as well have been.

The Road Not Taken
September 14, 2014

My dad always wanted me to be a pharmacist, or, if not a pharmacist, then a lawyer. Though he never said so directly, he never wanted me to be a writer, of that I am certain. And not because he didn't love literature. He read widely and he valued the written word, I think, as much as anyone. But pharmacy was a safe profession in his view; it had afforded him a good living (he and my Uncle Irv owned two thriving stores at one point), and it was only natural for him to want to pass this on.

I tried every conceivable way a teenager can to tell him I had no interest in the subject, but he was my dad, and he thought he knew me. Who knows? Maybe he thought he knew better than me. Fathers, I understand, can be overbearing like that sometimes. We went back and forth on this: he argued for the practicality of a life counting pills and chatting with people about their aches and pains; I kept saying, no thanks, it may be okay for you but I'd like to try something more romantic.

It's when I got a D in chemistry that he latched onto the bright idea of me being a lawyer. I was a fan of Perry Mason at the time, and so perhaps it was the opportune moment to pivot towards this possibility. Being a lawyer seemed not too far removed from being a detective, and I loved that idea. As it happened, I started visiting the Pasadena courthouse around then anyway, in part because it was summer and my friends and I were bored; also, it turns out, the courts were air-conditioned, and the theatrics were free. What I learned is that most folks on trial were poor and black or poor and Latino, and the cases we observed were middling, mind-numbing, penny-ante stuff: divorce, attempted burglary, vandalism, grand theft auto. Even with air-conditioning, that kind of wrangling kept us awake for maybe twenty minutes, tops.

Once, though, we almost hit the jackpot. That was the afternoon my friend David and I wandered into a packed courtroom and managed to find two seats towards the rear. A policeman was on the stand and we quickly surmised that not only was this a murder trial, it was an ax murder trial! How cool is that? The cop went on for about five minutes, then the judge's world-weary eyes scanned the crowd and all at once settled on us. "Uh, bailiff," he said, shaking his head and motioning in our direction, "will you please take the young men out?"

Everyone—and I mean everyone—turned to look at us. The bailiff, a burly, bald-headed fellow with a large gun on his holster, bore down upon us, and we melted away through the swinging doors. He was friendly enough once we were outside. "There's a pretty good accident case down the hall," he said by way of dismissal.

What's curious is that as my interest in the law began to wane, my father grew bored with pharmacy and at the tender age of sixty he went back to school. He wanted to be a lawyer, he declared. And the truth was he loved law school. He loved reading about torts and contracts; he was particularly fond of "con" law—constitutional law—with all its twists and turns. He was on a journey. He saw himself gaining wisdom in the sunset years of his life. He saw himself splitting hairs between justice and mercy, and it made him happy.

Then when he finally passed the bar, he joined a firm doing family law. That was the beginning of the end. "It's a slimy business," I warned him with my snarky sense of things. "Just you wait." And for him, it was true. He was now in a profession which forced him to dole out eviction notices and advise women who called him up at 2:00 A.M., telling him their husband was beating down the door, what should they do? After six months he quit the firm and started working for legal aid. But that wasn't much better. Most of his clients were drug dealers and multiple offenders, and, yes, they deserved a fair trial, but everyone (including my dad) knew they were guilty. And that fact by itself would have robbed him of any satisfaction if he ever managed to get them off the hook.

By the time we moved to Sonoma and started the bookstore, he was more than ready for retail again. Retail he understood. Retail made sense.

What You Don't Know
March 2008

At least once a week someone will come ambling through the door here, lean across the counter and feel the uncontrollable urge to confide in me that "I have always wanted to own a bookstore" or "when I retire from my dental practice, I'm going to run a bookstore" or "working in a bookstore is simply the best of all possible worlds."

From my point of view, the truth of these prospective booksellers' remarks is somewhat more nuanced—bookselling, like all retail, is subject to the riptides of an ever-changing market, as well as the day-to-day headaches of scheduling, inventory control, bill paying, etc.

But, in a broader sense, those who want to be booksellers are on to something. Owning a bookstore is a fantasy that (more or less) does what it purports to do. It does not, I hasten to add, make one a mountain of money, but there are other rewards: you get to put your hands on all the new, hot titles out there. You get to read books long before anyone else on your block, you get to be a minor pillar of the community, and, if you hold events, you get to schmooze with celebrities (well, sometimes with celebrities, but more often than not with authors, some of whom become celebrities, it's true, but mostly are just wonderful, witty people who end up obscure and bitter).

A lifetime ago, my wife and I were briefly involved in another popular fantasy—running a bed and breakfast in New England. Lots of folks then told us what a great time we must be having playing host to twenty stock brokers and their wives/mistresses a night (what diversity!), serving them home-made Hungarian coffee cake and fresh-squeezed orange juice every morning while regaling them with pithy stories of how we came to this quaint little burg and restored this quaint 18th century charmer of a home. We didn't tell them the downside of our fantasy—how we were virtually under house arrest all summer long, how our kids were bouncing off the walls because we never had time to be alone with them, how we both longed for a regular nine to five job where you didn't have to be on call every moment of the day. Let's just say that that was a fantasy that didn't work. Not for us, anyway.

Don't get me wrong—fantasies are important, and as Kafka said, we must be true to our dreams. But at the end of the day it is not simply the books sitting on the shelves that make this particular dream come true. It is the people who want them—need them—to complete some journey in their lives. It is the connection, the spark, that counts.

Yo Heave Ho
September 28, 2013

I've written so many of these essays now that I honestly can't remember if I've talked about this before. Probably so, but I don't care, surely it's worth another shot. Anyway, I want to speak about what we do at Readers' Books, and what I mean by that is not the lofty, civilizing tasks we engage in, like saving the planet and, with the help of literature, lifting our dispirited selves out of the primordial muck; that's all fine and good, and no one in his right mind could argue against it. No, the work I'm talking about, the real work, is far more mundane. What we do, day in and day out at Readers' Books, quite frankly, is schlep. "Schlep" is a Yiddish word. It means to tote or drag or haul, and if you know anything at all about the book trade, you know that, next to bricks, books are perhaps the heaviest things in the world; also, we schlep them relentlessly.

My dad was a master schlepper. During his time here he dutifully unpacked the books, checked them in, processed the returns, and hauled them in boxes—twenty, thirty, forty pounds each—to the post office. He did this for years and never took a penny in wages. That kind of worker is hard to find, let me tell you. We were impressed, so impressed in fact, that we once bought him an honorific sweat shirt with the words, FIELD MARSHAL IN CHARGE OF SHIPPING & RECEIVING, which is really just a fancy way of saying CHIEF SCHLEPPER. It didn't fit (too tight around the chest) but my dad was a sport and wore it anyway.

Today I schlepped some twelve boxes of books to the post office. A few of them were books that people had ordered and needed sent. One was to someone in prison. Sending books to folks in prison can be problematic: on the one hand, you're dealing with a captive audience; they have to pay for the book in advance and they're unlikely to be dissatisfied, no matter what you send them. On the other hand, the wardens at prisons sometimes act like Roman emperors. We've had books refused at prisons for no ostensible reason. And I once got a call from some clearly deranged cop in a high security lock up in Oklahoma who threatened to have me arrested for sending an inmate a book on Buddhist meditation. Did I know that books could contain knives or drugs? What were you thinking, boy? But that's another story. Most of the books I hauled up to the counter were returns, titles we'd taken a chance on, titles that no one in Sonoma had bought, worthy products whose authors had labored over for umpteen years, only to have them gather dust and eventually be schlepped into oblivion.

I used to fret over this process: the cycle between the hopeful receiving which inevitably leads, after a few short months, to the gloom of return. In between, we are supposed to sell these things, to talk them up, give them the gift of life, to make them seem essential to your well-being. Some of them are, of course, but only if you take the time and trouble to read them. And time is what no one has much of anymore.

Before we settled on Readers' Books as the store name, my favorite choice was Schleppers. I thought that kind of summed up what we do, but my wife, who is wiser than I will ever be, just shook her head. No one will understand, she said. I guess she's right. Big ideas are not my long suit. Give me a thirty pound box any day.

A Question for Anyone Out There
November 2007

My wife and I hold a business conference each morning in the car on our way to work. We do it in the car because that is virtually the only uninterrupted time we have together when we are both reasonably wide awake and neither one of us has yet committed a crime that would doom either of us to a day full of glares and silence. Also, we've discovered that in only about twenty minutes, you can actually solve some of life's riddles.

There is one riddle, though, that continues to elude us. How can it be, we wonder, that new fiction (which we sell by the ton and which is the essence of Readers' Books) does not attract a wider event audience? We can always get a crowd out for non-fiction and particularly for self-help speakers. Everyone, it seems, wants to know how to do their own divorce, lose weight, manage their panic attacks, avoid stalkers, massage their chakras, or get in touch with their intuitive inner child. But fiction? Well, that's a deeply personal affair. Now it's true, people do show up for celebrity fiction authors. Michael Chabon. Isabel Allende. Andre Dubus. These folks are excellent writers, to be sure, but they are also seen as established and we suspect that it is their celebrity status that is the big magnet. In fact, in our experience, a celebrity will trump just about anything when it comes to events.

The enigma (and the tragedy) is that new fiction is quite often the best and most interesting writing out there, but it only nets a handful of attention. A first-time novelist will pour his whole heart and soul into the story even if he/she has no idea if it will ever be published. The first-time novelist yearns to be read, he has a story to tell and he's always trying to hit one out of the park. Now of course you are "taking a chance" on a new novelist: not all of them are going to be stars. On the other hand, I would argue that the most moving experiences in one's reading life are invariably to be had in fiction. Fiction can make you laugh 'til your sides hurt; fiction can leave you shaking or in a puddle of tears. Fiction can make you stay up all night just to see how it ends. You won't get that kind of intensity in a book about a trip down the Seine or how to avoid carbohydrates.

I'm all in favor of non-fiction, mind you. We need to be informed. But we also need wisdom in our lives, and that sort of nourishment can only be found in stories and metaphors. At the end of the day, it is fiction that connects us to our humanity. We need to honor it always.

Small Pleasures
March 2006

My mother took pleasure in small things. Things that didn't cost a lot of money, things that nowadays seem almost quaint and sentimental. On rainy days she would gaze out the window and announce that it was a good day for making fudge. She liked to pack bunches of sandwiches and pile my brother and me and all the neighborhood kids into our old car for an afternoon at the beach. She loved to read. She would come home from the public library with so many books that her arms ached. Most of all she loved to play the piano. She played by ear, and would rip through the old standards, show tunes, folk songs, stuff from the Yiddish theater, one right after another, always at the same jaunty tempo. It didn't matter that one song was a waltz, another a lullaby; she had too much moxie to ever slow down. In the last twenty years of her life, she and my father played Scrabble virtually every night. They filled up several ringed notebooks with their scores. She rarely won, but, then, she didn't care. It was the game, the tea and cookies, the words that never appeared in any dictionary, but were allowed nonetheless. In short, the time well spent.

I think about this more now that she's gone, and I wonder about the small sentimental pleasures I indulge in. Is it possible, I think, that just sitting around noodling on my guitar is really the greatest thing I can aspire to? That in the end that's what life adds up to, after all?—a song? A little riff in B flat? I wonder too about the dream-world of books that I inhabit—as a writer, reader, and purveyor—how some books, for example, can mean so much to me at a given moment in my life, and then, should I reopen them ten or twenty years later, they mean something else entirely, or, worse, nothing at all.

When I was twelve, I remember buying a copy of Saroyan's *The Human Comedy* at our synagogue's annual rummage sale. It was a hardback and it cost a dime and when I was finished, I knew it was the best book I'd ever read. Years later, I sat down on the living room couch with my own two kids and that same copy of *The Human Comedy*, thinking they too would love it. Suffice it to say, they didn't. And while I still enjoyed it, Saroyan's universe of honest, hard-working, good-intentioned men and women caught up in a dark time now seemed rather distant and romantic. Rereading books is a dangerous occupation, of course, and maybe you can't go home again, as Thomas Wolfe once wrote. But more and more, I keep looking for those small pleasures to keep me company. Books, music, friends. Like my mother, that's what I seem to be gathering around me. And that's what seems to make all the difference.

On Putting It Into Focus
November 26, 2011

Someone sent me an email the other day asking what I am grateful for, which is a splendid question at any time of the year, but especially now. Apart from the usual things (children, family, friends, love, peace, marriage, health), I guess I would have to add a few intangibles: I am grateful for that last sweet Cole Porter tune I learned on the guitar, for that one special Jewish joke I told that made a customer of mine burst into laughter, for that moment, sitting by the wood stove after dinner with a book in my hand, when the house was warm and everything (I mean everything) was as it should be.

Pieces of the mosaic, small things that mean a lot.

Play It Again, Sam
July 13, 2013

Maybe because I've played guitar for over half a century, or because I like to bang out tunes on the piano, or maybe just because I care, I've always been uber conscious about what kinds of music wafts across our bookstore. You might not think that music matters much in retail, that music, or worse, Muzak, is everywhere nowadays, so why bother. It's true: you can hardly walk through any mall of any major city and not be accosted by Wayne Newton or Kenny G or some gloppy rendition of a Beatles tune. And you might be so saturated by this aural soup now that you've turned it all off; you no longer even think about it. Or, if you do think about it, you think it's just background and means, well, nothing.

Well, you'd be wrong. Music, to my ears anyway, means plenty. I've spent untold hours of my waking day and night trying to remember the chorus from "In a Sentimental Mood" or "Alone Together." And often when I'm driving my car, I'm also busy trying to work out the chord changes of one song or another. So yes, you could say I'm a little obsessive about music.

That said, I'm going to go out on a very short limb and argue that what one hears in a particular retail environment (a bookstore, for example) has a significant effect on one's experience and well-being. Years ago, I was given a CD from the movie of *The Mambo Kings Play Songs of Love*, which was based, of course, on Oscar Hijuelos' eponymous novel. I slid it into our CD player, pushed the start button and waited. A series of sprightly, very Cuban mambos came on. Shortly thereafter, a middle aged lady walked in the door. She stopped, startled perhaps by the trumpets and the syncopated drumming, made a face that could only signify confusion, turned on her heel and walked out. Needless to say, I took the CD off straight away and replaced it with Mozart.

Of course, not everyone wants to listen to a never-ending string of string quartets in a bookstore; like successful restaurants everywhere, you have to mix the menu up now and then to keep it interesting. But there are boundaries, things you cannot do and still stay in business. You cannot, for instance, play rap music or other such pounding and often salacious stuff—at least not in a bookstore where people come to think and explore and wonder about the universe. Neither is it a good idea to have too many protracted periods of silence. That causes nervousness and stultification—very bad. And while there are some staff members here who squirm at the idea of Edith Piaf or Bob Dylan, those artists are clearly within the canon; they work at a romantic, sub-atomic level; they help us summon specific memories from odd places in our brains. I have to say, I am always amazed by what books some people want to buy after hearing "Non Je Ne Regrette Rien" or "Ain't Gonna Work on Maggie's Farm No More."

I'm sure there's a lot more science on this topic, and it would probably be smart to read up on it, see if I could somehow, you know, get an angle on what really works. I'm not going to do that, however. Me, I just know what I like.

Are the Stars Out Tonight? I dunno...
October 13, 2011

We were driving around Chicago last month with our six year old grandson, Joe, in the backseat, when I asked Lilla something about my band, i.e., did she know when the next rehearsal was. Joe's ears perked up. You're in a band? he asked incredulously. Well, yeah, I said. I play the guitar. Joe thought about this for a moment. Are you the star of the band? he wanted to know. I shook my head. No, I said, not really. Well, said Joe, trying to put the best face on it, you know what they always say: The old guy in the band is never the star.

I've been thinking about that a lot lately. Fact is, I am the old guy in the band. On the other hand, I can name a number of old guys in bands (Willie Nelson, Mick Jagger, Elton John) who are the stars, so I don't know where he came up with that idea, except that six year old kids feel free to explore the whole universe in ways we older guys do not.

Joe is just starting out, of course. There is probably no way yet for him to fathom that being the most senior has some distinct advantages. One of the nice things, for example, about playing in this band is that I'm not trying to prove anything to anyone; when I play, it is simply to have fun. I am an amateur in the best sense of that word. If they pay us, fine. If they don't pay us, fine. For me, in the end, it's all about the music, which is kind of how I feel about books, too (and probably why I'm still waiting to make my first million).

Maybe to be a star you have to want something really bad, so bad you're willing to step all over other people to get there. And maybe if I've made it to the ripe old age I am and I'm still not a star, then I haven't done that. So in that sense, maybe Joe's right: The old guy in the band (at least this old guy) is never the star.

An Ode to Miss Stelgis
January 21, 2012

Before I became a world class guitarist (not), I took piano lessons—first from Miss Stelgis, at age five. I can't say I remember much about this phase of my musical life, only that my older brother was taught how to play boogie woogie while I was relegated to "Mary Had a Little Lamb" and similar gruel. Later on, when I was nine, I studied again with an elderly gentleman named Mr. Sinnett (neither Miss Stelgis nor Mr. Sinnett seemed to possess a first name, don't ask me why). This was a bit of an improvement, mainly because in addition to teaching me piano, Mr. Sinnett enjoyed playing chess. And more to the point, he wasn't very good at it, which meant that even when I stumbled over my Mozart and Brahms, I could almost always redeem myself on the field of battle.

The most terrifying experience of my young life took place at the keyboard, however: it was the day I had to take part in a recital. I remember the crowd of anxious parents and grandparents huddled in Mr. Sinnett's living room. I remember how uncomfortable I felt in my suit and tie (newly purchased from Sears), the beads of sweat forming on my prepubescent neck and forehead, the butterflies soaring around in my stomach. The piece was a Bach bouree, whatever that was, and somehow I forced myself through it at breakneck speed. I didn't care what it sounded like, I didn't care about anything except getting it over with and melting back into the wallpaper. In retrospect, the only good thing about the whole performance was that I wasn't required to speak. That, I am quite sure, would have killed me on the spot.

Fear of public speaking ranks right up there with fear of death, illness, loss of livelihood, and losing one's mind. Every child has had to deal with public speaking, of course, and most get through it, though few of us ever seem to relish it. For me, it was particularly petrifying. Whenever I had to be in a school play I would ask to be an extra, a third spear carrier perhaps, or a busboy. Nothing with lines. I remember my mother counseling me once about an upcoming public appearance (it might have been my bar mitzvah): "Just think of them all," she said, "as a bunch of cabbage heads." God knows I tried. I stood up on there on the stage, I squinched my eyes and tried to imagine, but it turned out in the end I was just as terrified of cabbage heads as human ones.

What's fascinating now is that after twenty years of introducing authors in front of crowds, there's little to be afraid of anymore. You may not believe this, but I don't even think much about what I'm going to say when I step in front of a microphone; it just comes out willy nilly and no one seems to notice. (Well, okay, maybe they notice but are just too polite to say something.) To be honest, I don't know how I managed to cure myself. Maybe aging and experience has made me a better person, at least in this one regard. Or maybe I just don't care anymore. To me, my newfound ease with public speaking is still a miracle, not unlike those I used to watch on TV, where crippled people suddenly threw down their crutches and walked. All I know is today I can stand before an audience and my knees won't quake. I don't have to read from a yellow legal pad. I can think and speak clearly. Sometimes, people tell me, I'm even funny. Which is a good thing, because why would anyone come to a bookstore in order to be bored? You wouldn't. Neither would I. Funny helps. As does my fearlessness (carelessness?) at the podium. Those stultifying hours at the piano: I have to give them credit, too. It all adds up. So thank you, Miss Stelgis, wherever you are.

The Answer is Never What You Think It Is
March 2011

One of the most critical and least understood questions on the job application form here at Readers' Books is the following: If stranded on a desert island, what book or books would you want to have with you?

When I included this question it was never meant to be literal: that is to say, it's not about you and a desert island, though occasionally we do get applicants who think so. If he or she puts down, "A book about how to build a raft," I generally take that to mean I'm dealing with a plodder, a basic nuts-and-bolts, let's just put-one-foot-in-front-of-the-other kind of person, someone who thinks only in concrete terms and who therefore will never get the kinds of jokes I tell all day long, so why would I want to work with them in the first place?

If, however, they write down *"Don Quixote,* or the longest book I can find" I might conclude that this person is overly adept at sitting back and doing nothing, just waiting for his or her boat to come in. I wouldn't say the word "lazy," though it would always be lurking in the back of my mind. This is also not a promising sign.

There are some people who put down only the books they have read before, usually what was assigned to them in high school. I have problems with that answer too, because you see, I remember what I had to read in high school, and what I remember most vividly was that, for the most part, I hated those books. Dickens, Hawthorne, Dostoevsky—they're not such bad writers, but when you're sixteen, and your face looks like a pizza, and your hormones are tap dancing all over your body day and night, and someone your mother's age is making you plod through this stuff, how can you possibly like it? Okay, you might be able to endure it, but like it? Really? And not only that, you're telling me now you actually want to take it to read over again on a desert island? C'mon.

Lately, with the job market tighter than ever, I've noticed that more applicants are looking for an academic or rarified impression with their book choices. *"Shakespeare's Tragedies* (the Folger Editions)" or "the *Oxford English Dictionary* (all 27 volumes)." And in the same vein, a few folks opt for the old spiritual stand-bys that have worked well for prisoners in the past—the *King James Bible* or *The Golden Bough* or Suzuki's *Zen Buddhism.* These are not bad choices, I suppose, but they suggest that the applicant is either struggling way too hard to impress his future boss, or else he or she needs to try something more daring, like sky-diving or internet dating.

Of course there is no right answer to what book you would bring to a desert island. I mean, it's really a stupid question when you think about it. My favorite response of all was the most whimsical. A fellow put down "*The Story of Ferdinand*—because it is quite clearly the best book ever written." He didn't take it seriously. Him I hired on the spot.

Transiency
May 16, 2015

Not so long ago, I lived in a house with a million books. Well, not a million, okay. But lots and lots. There were so many books that we named the place where we lived Book Farm, which was, of course, a play on Brook Farm, which probably didn't have so many books, but never mind. There were so many books at Book Farm that many shelves were piled two-deep. There were so many books that the stacks seemed to form structural supports for the ceiling. And, naturally, the fact of so many books made for very well insulated winter nights.

I was happy at Book Farm. I could look at my multitude of books—some read, some unread, some never to be read, some gathered for a reason long forgotten—and think that this was what civility looked like, this was the essence of a cultured life, this was why mankind had made the long, hard struggle out of the primitive slime in the first place.

Now, however, my circumstances have changed radically. For one thing, we no longer own a house. We have moved several times in the past year or two. I won't bore you with the details, but suffice it to say that we are now living out of our suitcases. This is not forever, nor is it necessarily a bad thing. We are not homeless so much as "between" houses. And this lack of permanence has benefits we never before considered: for instance, when a friend suggested the other night that we might be interested in purchasing one of his mother's paintings, before we could even respond, someone else cheerfully pointed out that we no longer had walls. This not only made our friend feel stupid, it elicited all kinds of sympathy for our plight.

But the truth is, it's not so bad. In fact, I've come to realize that the biggest perk I have as a bookseller is the knowledge that I don't have to own any given book. Or, put another way: almost any book I want I can probably lay my hands on quickly, and at cost, so why create another Book Farm? Though books are lovely to look at, there are surely cheaper forms of insulation.

I'm not saying you should stop buying books—heaven forbid! The world goes on spinning, and folks are forever dreaming up new and vital stories we need to know about. Without books and the good folks who write them we are doomed.

It's that simple and that stark: Books are the engines that move us forward.

But at the moment, as I said, I'm in transit, which means I have just a few books I'm currently working my way through. That's more than enough. They fit nicely on the night stand. I can read them simultaneously. And though one day soon I'll start collecting them again and watch them pile up around me like errant children, for now it's pleasant to focus on one or two as if they contained the entire universe within their covers. And who knows? Maybe they do.

Property is Theft
June 16, 2012

Growing up as they did during the Great Depression, my late father and father-in-law were, unsurprisingly, both devout seekers of bargains. Any piece of paper marked "sale" was sure to catch their eye, and even though through a combination of luck and hard work they both achieved a remarkable degree of solvency, there always remained a special place in their hearts for that electric thrill that comes over you when you get a "steal."

I have nothing against bargains or bargain hunting, but I was always amazed at the lengths they would go to in order to score. George, Lilla's dad, used to go to a vast discount emporium called Fedco (think Walmart, without the charm) and come home with the damnedest things. Once, for example, he arrived with something like ten pounds of Gummy Bears in his arms, not because he ate them, but they were so cheap, how could he possibly resist? And even though my parents lived in a small mobile home and didn't eat much, my dad was forever stocking up on Safeway's nifty two-for-one deals. Two giant boxes of raisin bran for the price of one, two 5 pound boxes of Oreos, two this, two that. My brother and I were continually inheriting this extra stuff they didn't need, didn't eat, and didn't know what to do with.

Bargains are tricky things is my point, I suppose. One must be ever conscious of when a bargain mysteriously crosses a line and becomes all at once a burden. Lately, for instance, I have had wonderful luck at a certain thrift shop in town. A few months ago I walked in and scored three different sports coats there: total price $8. Can you beat that? No, you can't. It's a miracle. On the other hand, it turns out I don't actually need three more sports coats (I now own six, which is beyond crazy.) And I didn't even grow up in the Depression, so I can't blame it on latent subliminal anxieties or the fear that history will repeat itself. I am my father's son, however. So...do you think this might be genetic? Lord, I hope not. I stopped eating Oreos years ago, so maybe it's not so bad. Maybe there's hope, or a cure on the horizon....how much can that cost?

My World, and Welcome to It
July 2009

My father thought of himself as a failure. He dreamed of becoming a doctor, probably to offset the helplessness he felt as a twelve year-old boy watching his own father die. That proved to be too lofty a goal, however, and after many years at many different jobs he settled for becoming a pharmacist, a career at which he made a decent living. Still, for him at least, the glass was always half empty. In his view, he had failed.

Failure is rather like beauty, of course—in the eye of the beholder. It need not revolve around money and prestige. You could argue (and I did) that because he married the love of his life, raised two talented sons, lived long enough to see his four grandchildren come of age and did many other good deeds along the way, that my father did pretty well. He would have argued back, but you see what I mean.

I grew up thinking I would be a fiction writer someday, a vague cross perhaps between Raymond Chandler, Albert Camus, and Yasunari Kawabata. That didn't pan out, and once in a while, in spite of my best efforts, I can't help but feel as though I too "settled," becoming a "mere" bookseller. This is of course a misreading of history; things happen, events conspire one way or another, and presto—there you are, selling books to the masses.

The far larger truth is that I was lucky. And I know now from years of watching and listening to famous writers that the road they travel down is not nearly so smooth as I once believed. Real writers lead lonely, frustrating lives. They stare at computer screens for hours and hours, and at the end of the day they wonder whether they've produced anything at all. Real writers (unless they teach at a college or wait tables) are often impoverished. Real writers know humiliation. Unless they are born celebrities, they have to stand beside espresso machines at places like Borders and read their opening chapters aloud to two or three hapless employees on their lunch break. Real writers cruise bookstores like ours hoping their titles are still on the shelves and fearing they've all been sent back to the publishers to be crushed into paving material. Real writers, in the end, are at war: with their editors, their agents, their audiences, the media, and ultimately, with themselves.

By contrast, I inhabit a tranquil place, a delightful world filled with beauty and wisdom: books come in, books go out. Grand ideas, not such grand ideas, all swirling around at a polite distance. It's like being in the eye of a hurricane, I think. And if I have settled for anything at all it is this: a calm, sane, and civilized landscape.

What I Say to Al
May 2009

One of the principle joys of owning a bookstore is that it enables you to participate in the political debates of the day. Last week, for example, a friend of mine—I'll call him Al—told me that he is taking all his money out of American stocks and buying into the emerging Chinese and Indian markets. Al was discouraged, to put it mildly—actually he was apoplectic—about the financial meltdown now in progress. And despite the recent spate of "good behavior" on Wall Street he continues to insist that the sky is falling on America.

Al is a smart guy. He knows business and can speak fluent economics. He's also made a lot of money in life (far more than I'll ever see, I'm sure) and so when he says the winds are shifting sharply toward the Orient I am inclined to listen. Not agree, but listen.

On the other hand, I say when he pauses to take a breath, as an armchair historian I know that economists have predicted twelve of the last nine recessions in this country so their overall track record is—how shall we put it—spotty? Still, Al has a point. China and India, long dormant, are on the move. They are growing their economies by leaps and bounds, while here in the USA we've watching GM hand out pink slips as though they are confetti, malls are vanishing, and some folks are living in their cars (until those get repossessed as well). Chinese bond holders, says Al, are all that's keeping us from going completely over the cliff.

True enough, I reply. But what is true now economically does not necessarily mean it will be true forever or even two years down the road. In the early 30's many of my parents' contemporaries openly admired the Soviet Union, in no small part because it seemed to provide employment for everyone. That was before the purges and the famines and the gulags in Siberia. And remember the 50's and 60's when everyone was yammering about all the leisure time we were going to enjoy, thanks to the wonders of technology? Remember the Monsanto House of the Future in Disneyland? That place where everything operated by push button? Remember the leisure suit? If you can't remember any of these things, don't worry: that was then, this is now.

What I say to Al is that there's one thing that always trumps economics, and that's history. China and India are wonderful places, but they have problems—big historical, political, linguistic, cultural, religious, and economic problems that have, at least for the last 5,000 years, been pretty intractable.

In China, for example, the vast majority of people are illiterate farmers who earn maybe a dollar a day. Now it's true that in the last few years tens of millions of them have migrated to the cities to work in the local hula hoop factory where they make a glorious twenty bucks a day. But what happens when we stop buying hula hoops and that factory shuts down? What are those folks going to do? They aren't going back to the farm. The farm may not even be there anymore. And the Chinese government just doesn't have the flexibility, or any mechanism at all really, for dealing with that many idle, angry workers. Oh, yeah, I forgot, they can send in the Red Army! That's the ticket.

What I say to Al is that, historically, people have always lost money when they bet against America. I know we're in a global nightmare at the moment, but if anyone is going to emerge from this rapidly, it is us. We have all the ingredients to succeed. We like to innovate. We are inherently pragmatic. We don't have much of a past to think about, let alone be paralyzed by. The Chinese, the Indians, even the Europeans, are, au contraire, hemmed in by their history.
What I say to Al is that we just elected the first person of color as President. You won't see that happening in Germany or England. And China doesn't bother holding elections; they've always favored civil wars instead.

What I say to Al is wait. Just wait.

Who was that Masked Man?
May 10, 2014

Viewed through the lens of a passing satellite miles above the earth, some people might suppose that Sonoma is just a typical little town—another Peoria, a pleasant place utterly devoted to the pursuit of the ordinary. Well, I'm here to disabuse you of that notion. Some people would be wrong. Sonoma is not an ordinary town. How do I know? It's simple, really. I know because (and you'll forgive me if I sound loopy) the truth is this town is populated by angels. Or, okay, if you're one of those who don't believe in angels, if you lean toward more Eastern types, this town is populated by bodhisattvas—folks who have attained enlightenment, but instead of floating off into the ether, are still hanging around, loitering here on earth, as it were, to do social good. This is my firm belief. And if anyone ever took it upon themselves to do an angel/bodhisattva census I'd bet Sonoma would rank right up there with...well, the angels.

We had an angel visit us last week, in fact. A woman was at the counter of the bookstore making a purchase, when she noticed our employee bulletin board. The message at the top was a heads-up for all the staff: we had recently been given a counterfeit hundred dollar bill, which no one noticed at the time, and which I blithely tried to deposit at the bank. The bank, for some reason, looks askance at phony money; they snatched up the bill and announced that they would be handing it over directly to the FBI, who deal with such things. Which meant, of course, that I, the lowly merchant, had been snookered, and was now out one hundred bucks. What will the FBI do? I asked, ever hopeful. Oh, nothing probably, said the bank teller. They just collect them. (Her point being, I was never going to see my money again, and I should just get over it).

So, in light of this event, we posted an alert to all our employees to check whatever large bills we get for their bogusness. And this woman saw the notice and out of the kindness of her heart, gave us another hundred dollars, just like that. Now, you could always chalk this up to karma—what goes around comes around, etc.—only that takes the personal agency out of the equation, makes it all into a strange, unknowable cosmic clock: you know, things out of balance just go back into balance on their own, that's the way of the universe. Well no, I don't think so. Maybe I'm just an incorrigible romantic, but I want to believe there's justice in the world, and that justice doesn't come magically from on high; justice is something rendered only by people rising to the occasion.

So this woman walked in and handed us a hundred dollars to compensate for our loss. And I need to thank this woman for her random act of kindness. After all, she had no idea she was going to spend that extra cash when she walked in; it must have surprised her as well. I don't know her, and she left no note behind for me to read. There one minute and gone the next, like the Lone Ranger. You can call that justice if you like. But she, whoever she was, can clearly be called an angel.

Some Words that Need to Be Said
June 11, 2011

The following should perhaps be filed either under "the bonds of friendship" or my compulsive need to "put a human face on whatever it is we do." In any case, it's part of my world now, and even though it is not, strictly speaking, about Readers' Books, I still feel obliged to acknowledge it publicly.

Some very tragic news to report: Two weeks ago one of our dear old comrades in the book business ended her life by jumping off the Golden Gate Bridge. All her many friends on Facebook are busy recounting the zany and wonderful things about her (and there were many); they are raising their glasses on her behalf (and they should); they are saying prayers and planning a memorial (good idea). But these are at best, gestures. What strikes me most is the size of the void left by anyone's passing. How death—no matter how it happens—sends out pulses of pain in all directions. And the fact that this person died well before her time, in such an awful and dramatic way, only adds to the anguish.

All of us are wondering now, is there anything we could have done? We all knew she was depressed; we all knew that her big smiles and funny jokes came out of a place of immense sadness. But what is truly sad is that without her to give voice to them, there are no answers. Someone we loved and valued, someone we saw regularly, year in and year out, ate lunch with, laughed with, partied with, is gone. That's all. And now we are left only with this persistent pain, this emptiness beyond any scientific or religious explanation, which we know will pass, but not for a long, long time.

The Lesson of September
September 2008

Every year when September rolls around on the calendar I decide that it's time once again to take stock. Of course a lot of folks do this in January, but in my view that's a mistake. How can you possibly look at your life rationally when Christmas and New Year's leaves you broke and worn out and hung over? I'll tell you how—you can't. Or rather, you can, but invariably you'll learn the wrong lessons from the errors of your ways. You'll put yourself on a grapefruit diet, you'll cancel all your magazine subscriptions, you'll resolve never to eat out again. This is wrong, because the truth about January is that in January everyone is poor and worn out and numb, and no amount of atonement is going to change your condition. No, the lesson of January is that you must wait patiently until spring. Bears know this. Can humans be that far behind? Which leads me back to September.

In September we sense the seasons starting to turn, and we welcome the hint of coolness and the prospect of rain. In September the school year begins again, with all its hope for a new generation of intelligent young people who will not wreck the planet the way their forebears did. Here in the bookstore September means "the season" when all the publishers in New York trot out their new titles and all their authors start showing up in places like ours. There are shiny new books on the shelves, and brave and interesting people to amuse and instruct us. It is, you might say, a brave new world, though a far, far happier one than Aldous Huxley might have imagined.

In September, too, I think about our friends and neighbors, how supportive they've been and how much we rely on them (you, that is) for our continued well-being. Good things have happened to us, after all. Less than twelve months ago Readers' Books was named Business of the Year. Last July (with help from our friends at the Sonoma Community Center and many others) we launched The Reading Garden. By the end of the summer we had the foundation of a delightful patio garden behind the bookstore. Beauty emerged from what was once rubble. This collaboration has done a lot for us, and I hope it has done at least as much to nourish the community. The lesson I've learned from September is that we are all in this together and whenever we take a step—even a small one—to uplift one another, well sir, we lift up the whole world.

On the Care and Feeding of Readers
February 28, 2015

The readers of the Sun have just awarded us an honored place in their pantheon. Readers' Books apparently renders the "best customer care" in the Valley. We, of course, cannot help but agree, although the meaning of best customer care is open to interpretation. We're gratified that you have noticed this care, and find it so valuable as to give us an award for it. We appreciate that you notice what we're trying to do; it makes us feel loved and cared for as well. So, thank you.

For sure, we care about our customers, but to be fair, so does every other store on our block. However, our care extends beyond wanting them to keep coming into our store forever, rain or shine. If we had our druthers, we'd like them to live long, healthy, and happy lives. We'd also dearly like their lives to be meaningful (whatever that means), full of curiosity and endless excursions down the many byways of literature, history, memoir, and more.

Being a bookstore gives us a natural leg up on many of our would-be competitors, I imagine. I mean, there's a vast difference between selling you a fantastic novel—something that will irrevocably change your whole life's direction—and, say, making a great pepperoni pizza or doing a boffo job on your muffler. Not that there's anything wrong with pizza or fixing mufflers; we sort of need those things in our lives (well, maybe not pizza so much if it gives you heartburn). The Sun gave its readers a number of categories to choose from, some more critical than others. Let us all admit, for example, that pizza is rarely a game-changer. You eat it, or you don't. In the big scheme of things it doesn't matter; your life will go on regardless. But a book, as we've said many times before, can be an altogether different animal. A book can start a new religion or spark a revolution. A book can topple governments or move national boundaries. A book can lead the way to heaven or hell. When I show up at the post office with a box of books, I am always asked, do you have anything that's liquid, perishable, or potentially hazardous inside? And I always want to say, liquid or perishable, no. Hazardous? You bet.

That said, it's true that we care about our customers. We care about what they read, that they are able to read whatever they desire, and that books--hazardous or not--are always within their reach. I guess you could call that care. It's what we do.

Read Your Vegetables
December 7, 2013

I have a good friend, a cultured, intelligent woman I've known for nearly half a century, who never reads fiction. Nothing wrong with that, I think. She's read a good deal of fiction growing up, of course—Dickens and Proust and Margaret Atwood and Barbara Kingsolver—but in the end, she always finds the bulk of it unsatisfying. Facts, she says, are what animate her, facts and ideas (which are kind of like facts, only they're rather invisible to the naked eye, except when you see them in the Sunday funnies). Anyway, this friend of mine and I got to discussing things, and this notion that fiction is just stories, and untrue stories besides, reared its head again, and it made me wonder whether the world might just divide along those lines, and whether people who only read one or the other are missing something vital.

I read both fiction and nonfiction (history and memoir in the main) but to me, fiction is simply another way of telling the truth. When you read Louise Erdrich's *The Round House*, you're pulled into a whole world of American Indian experience, much of it painful to consider, but true. And in *Dissident Gardens*, when Jonathan Lethem talks about the angst of New York Jews and the social issues that turned some of them into Communists, he is describing a very real circumstance in people's lives. There are facts that underlie both of these stories, but these facts only come alive in the hands of a gifted novelist. And, by the same token, a book like Peter Baker's *Days of Fire: Bush and Cheney in the White House* paints a revealing portrait of the officials in charge and what motivated them. They are real human beings, with all the faults and strengths and eccentricities of human beings, but because they were involved in the drama of the time, it's also not a reach to see them as characters.

This holiday season, then, I strongly suggest you dip into both fiction and nonfiction. There is an abundance of great new writing out there. You can regard it the same way you look at eating—a little of this, a little of that. You know, balanced.

Book Stars
November 2009

I have long believed that the need to be part of the larger continuum is just as compelling as the need to cut one's own path to fame and fortune. Nothing wrong with fame and fortune, mind you, except that they say it's a tad lonely at the top. Belonging to a continuum, on the other hand, has its own headaches, but at least you always have someone else around to give you a high five or a shoulder to cry on or a great idea that will send you venturing into space.

Last Christmas, we came up with just such an idea that we think is so wonderful, we want to add it to the continuum of our holiday season.

We call it Book Stars and here's how it works: When you come in to do your Christmas or Hannukah shopping, we're hoping you will take a moment to add one or two extra kid's books to your purchases—any kid's book for any age, in any language, any price, you choose—and we will sort it and send it along to one of the local charities listed below in time for the holidays.

The rewards for this random act of kindness are threefold: 1) you get to give some child or young person in a difficult situation the joy of reading; 2) you add your voice to the defense of local independent book selling and to the fabric of our community; and 3) your yellow or blue star will be hung on our wall for all to see. Then, on New Year's Day, at our giant annual "no football, Bloody Mary, free aspirin" blowout sale, we will draw two lucky stars to receive $50 gift certificates. There is, of course, no limit to the number of stars (books) you can buy in this regard. One star is wonderful; ten stars—hey you're a constellation of your own.

This year, we have selected The Teen Center, La Luz, Sonoma Overnight Shelter (SOS), and the Teen Parent Program as recipients. In addition, we're including donations to Seeds of Learning, which, while it is a national nonprofit group, has a strong local chapter in town. Seeds of Learning sponsors teams of good-hearted folks who go down to El Salvador and Nicaragua each year to build schools in rural areas. It just so happens that Sonoma's own Sara Donnelly has written a great bilingual children's book (Esperanza and the New School) and proceeds from it will go directly to Seeds of Learning, so we thought it was a natural "fit" with our stars idea.

Last year, even in the teeth of the recession, we managed to give away over 700 books this way. Imagine what we can do in 2009.

Why Mysteries Matter
January 26, 2013

Each month, a woman of a certain age comes into our store with a paper bag full of mysteries she has read and wishes to trade in. She always leaves with that same bag filled with more mysteries, a never-ending cycle as it were. As I watched her go out with her new treasure, it got me to thinking about the nature of mysteries. Why do so many people love them? It's not about the violence, I've decided; there are plenty of straight-ahead fiction books filled with far worse violence. Nor is it the tragedy of someone killed in some gruesome manner and the effect of this on his or her loved ones, though that can certainly be a part of a mystery. No, what makes mysteries so appealing is that they are, in the end, morality plays wrapped in labyrinths.

Someone is killed, and in order to recreate justice and balance in the world, someone else needs to determine what happened. Once that is done, the world is a better place, or, at any rate, a safer place for the time being. Occasionally, the seeker is a relative or a bystander—the school librarian or the small town doctor. Then there are the professional seekers, the Philip Marlowe or Sam Spade detectives we've come to know over the years, burnt out cases who can somehow use their compass to point faithfully towards the truth, even when pickled in alcohol. When we read a mystery, then, we (the armchair detective) get to feel good about our rational skills and about a world where fairness and clarity are abide. That's a good thing.

Everyone, I think, should experience that kind of happiness.

I am Bookseller, Hear Me Roar
February 11, 2012

In the course of any given day, I am asked at least a dozen times, "Have you read this book?" Sadly, the answer is almost always no, no, of course not, I mean, there are 18,000 books in this store, for Pete's sake, look around you, it's practically raining books. How in God's name could I possibly read them all, let alone the one you're holding in your hands?

Okay, I don't say this. Usually I just say "no" or "no, not yet" and leave off with all the snarkiness. Occasionally it turns out, I have read the book in question. Or at least a chapter of the book. Or a page. Or, if I really didn't care for it, the first sentence. I know that it's wrong to treat writing this way. In particular, it's patently cruel to the author, who has spent perhaps the better part of three years slaving over this thing in some cramped, unheated room upstairs, writing away while his wife was down in the kitchen chopping vegetables filled with resentment and his kids considering him an airhead. I know the only reason he kept on, the only reason he persisted with it, was because his agent in New York assured him that this book would fundamentally alter the arc of civilization. I know, I know. I was once delusional like F. Scott Fitzgerald (well, not like F. Scott Fitzgerald, but delusional, you bet). The only difference was he got published and I did not.

I am not sad about this. It's just what it is. Sometimes (not often, but once in a while) I am even relieved not to be a famous author. I think of how they are pushed around mercilessly like pawns, all the pressure from those multiple yearbook contracts, the film rights, the foreign rights, the long overseas flights in cramped seats, the speaking engagements, the obscenely rich food you have to eat, and those lonely nights in silent, post-modern, air-conditioned 5 star hotels.

And I think: Do I still really want that? Wouldn't I rather be right here in the bookstore, in my old cardigan sweater, sipping tea and telling people this is a good book, you need to read this before you die. Or better yet—this book was terrible—terrible!—it was so bad I read two pages and threw it against the wall. Now that, that, my friend, is power.

Something Borrowed, Something Blue
March 24, 2012

We have been gathering and recycling used books for over a dozen years now, and when you've done the same task, day in and day out, for that long, well, let's just say certain things become clear. For one, you don't know it, but most of you are reading the same books as everyone else. Oh, you may think you have an eccentric and well-balanced literary diet, but the truth is, you are consuming ungodly amounts of the same six authors everyone else is reading. Now, that said, it's not such a terrible thing that you like Stieg Larsson or Jodi Picoult or Alice Hoffman. In fact, you could argue that because you are giving them back to us to dispose of, you are different than the rest of the planet. You have moved on to loftier realms of literature. Oh sure, you may have deigned to read them once, but that was then and this is now. Brain candy, be gone. Okay. Except that almost all of you are still doing this, and we keep seeing the same six authors, for which, as you may imagine, we have only limited shelf space or interest.

Another thing we couldn't help noticing is that really good reads tend to be the ones that are most damaged by the time they land on our counter. They are bent and bedraggled and coffee-stained. Some have been snatched away and chewed on by envious pets, and more than a few have been inadvertently dropped in bath water. The not-so-great titles are usually pristine, because, after all, who would possibly read them?

Once in a very long while, we'll get to sort through the leavings of an odd and otherworldly fellow. This can be an amazing experience, but most often all we get is just the slightest glimpse of his/her penchants and passions—a volume of Aleister Crowley's poetry or a book on how to shoot arrows like a Zen master or a Jungian's take on what was the really the matter with Hitler. (What was the matter with Hitler, anyway?) Book people like that almost never surrender their most precious titles; alas, we are perpetually dealing with their dregs and left to wonder what splendid jewels still remain on their shelves. Such is life.

Books and Fate
September 4, 2015

What I love about books is that they do not sit still. They may look still, and, from a certain angle, even inert. But they are not. Often, whenever I finish a book that particularly moves me, I pass it on to someone else. Sometimes it is a "loan" and meant to be returned. And sometimes that happens, but often both the lender and the lendee lose track of it. It's a book, after all, not your grandmother's diamond necklace. You forget, they forget. It's okay. Years go by. They move to a smaller house. The book is put in a box with other books. It gathers dust in a garage and on a fine spring day it goes for fifty cents in a yard sale to someone else. The journey continues.

Last week, I was asked by Muriel Robbins' daughter, Pam, to come over and sort through her late mother's books. Muriel Robbins, as most of you know, was an iconic figure in Sonoma. She was the daughter of Helen Shainsky and part of that group of pioneering Jews, many of them Zionists and socialists, who came to Sonoma around the turn of the last century and went into the chicken business. Muriel was also kind of a relative of mine (don't ask me to parse the exact relationship); she was the aunt or the cousin or the niece of my cousin Charlie's first wife, Carol. I think we both attended the wedding, though that was a long time ago and Charlie and Carol have long ago moved on to other spouses, but never mind. Muriel became close friends/relations with my parents when they moved to Sonoma. They used to get together to eat and tell Yiddish jokes, and so for all the time I've known her she has been "mishpuchah"—family.

I was going through her shelves, picking things that might be worthwhile, when I came across a copy of an old out-of-print book I read years ago called *Words Like Arrows*. It's a collection of Yiddish sayings and insults. Some of the adages are wise, a few reflect the bitterness and narrow world forced upon Jews living in the ghettoes of Eastern Europe, and many are just plain hilarious. One of my favorites is "Er hot in di hoyzn a yarid," which is actually a reference to syphilis, and translates to "He has a carnival in his pants."

There were several boxes of usable titles, and the next day, as I was categorizing and pricing them I came upon that book again and opened it. On the front page was an inscription. It read: "April 11 is one of the best days there is, don't you agree." This startled me because April 11 happens to be my birthday. Then I noticed more writing below. "Happy birthday, Andy." And then I recognized the signature of an old buddy of mine from New England. And, slow-witted though

I am, I finally put together what happened. This was my book originally. I must have passed it on to my parents, who forget where it came from and passed it on to Muriel.

And now, years later, after all those folks have vanished from the earth, it's home again in my living room. In Yiddish they would call this sequence of events "besheret"—meant to be. And I'm sure if I look hard enough in *Words Like Arrows*, I'll find an even juicier expression for it.

Here's What's Happening on Our Block
April 6, 2013

Sometime in the middle of April, my friend Steve Blackmer will close the door of his antiquarian bookshop, Chanticleer, climb into his used Volvo, and drive home. And a few days or weeks later another enterprise will open there. The good news is that he is not—like Sonoma Bookends—going out of business. Steve was approached by a couple of antiquarian book lovers from Walnut Creek who wanted to buy his inventory. He is going to keep the core books, however, the ones he loves to sell, and continue as an online presence. This is eminently reasonable: Most of his business is conducted over the internet anyway, and although he has enjoyed meeting customers face to face, one can understand why he might not want to keep paying the rent and the light bill after all these many years.

Still, I have to say it saddens me that he's leaving. It was nice having another interesting bookshop across the street to refer folks to, and Steve, who has been in the book business far longer than me, was always someone easy to sit around and chew the fat with. Moreover, Chanticleer and Readers' Books and all the other curiosities of East Napa Street were part of a larger mosaic, a beautiful old-fashioned neighborhood with a special, indescribable magnetism. That's now diminished a bit. We're still here, of course, and our intention is to stay here, but now we're really, truly the only bookstore left in town.

I don't pretend to know how to manage change, let alone stop it altogether. I don't even think that's something to be desired. And maybe we will never reach a consensus as to what we'd like our planet to look like, what businesses to keep, how high the skyline should be, that kind of thing. Manhattan was once small and semi-rural too, remember. And, in medieval times, packs of wolves appeared regularly at the gates of Paris, imprisoning the terrified inhabitants.

So going backward is not an option. But going forward by simply letting the market decide is, to my mind at least, a cop out, an abandonment of who we are as thoughtful, caring human beings. When someone dies, we weep. When someone leaves, we wish them well and wave goodbye.

What They Said. Or Should Have.
March 2013

My old and now sadly departed friend, Charlie Cooke, used to come into the bookstore every few days to while away the afternoon in our history section. He was, in my view, the perfect patriot. He read voraciously. He was engaged in the issues of the day and informed on all the latest news. He'd spent a good deal of his life in the military and in government service, and he did not suffer fools gently. He loved to swear and to argue. He loved the fact that for a brief moment Nixon suspected him of leaking the Pentagon Papers. And, most of all, he loved to call out the modern Republican establishment for their failure to live up to their own stated beliefs.

Charlie always carried a copy of the U.S.Constitution around in his shirt pocket. He knew it pretty well, but I suspect he kept it just in case he walked into a bar and needed extra black and white evidence to bolster his point of view. I've been giving some thought to that document lately, and, while it is brilliant in many respects, it also contains a serious—and I believe, unreported— flaw. You see, the Constitution offers Americans all kinds of rights, but it doesn't generally demand that we do anything for them. No, rights are "God given" and "inalienable," as it is said. Like sunshine or rain, nothing much you can do about it.

But what if, along with the Bill of Rights, came an equally sacred Bill of Responsibilities? What if the Founders took it upon themselves to suggest that Americans must act like grown ups? That's the way it ought to have been stated. You have the right to free speech, for example, but you cannot yell "Fire!" in a crowded theater. You have the right to bear arms, but you must rigorously commit to keeping that firearm out of an irrational person's hands. And the right to bear arms doesn't mean you have the right to own weapons so powerful they can decimate a whole town. You have the right to worship as you please, but your religious beliefs cannot, under any circumstances, impugn or limit the beliefs of others. You have the right to vote, but you are obliged to educate yourself about the candidates and what they would do if elected. As we've seen all too often recently, an electorate that lets itself be led around by the nose, an electorate that doesn't ask questions and demand answers, isn't serving democracy; it's aiding the interests of lobbyists.

A lot of this reasoning has been hammered out in the courts over the last several hundred years. And some is obviously still going on. But wouldn't it have been nice if, in their infinite wisdom, the guys who started the whole idea of America recognized that while we cherish our individualism, we're all in this wilderness together, and that means we have to come up with a simple, reciprocal, straight-forward way to get along? Other countries have done this; it shouldn't really be that hard. With rights come responsibilities. That's the whole thing in a nutshell. I never got a chance to run this by Charlie Cooke, but if he were still around today I feel pretty damn sure he'd agree.

Bert and Ernie
July 2013

This week's cover (July 8th) of The New Yorker magazine brought a smile to my face. It also got me thinking. If you haven't yet seen it, the cover shows an old black and white television, the kind I grew up watching, complete with rabbit ears. On the screen the full U.S. Supreme Court is posed, as if for a photo op, while in the foreground, watching perhaps from a couch, we see the faint, but clearly discernible outlines of two legendary Sesame Street characters, Bert and Ernie. You can only catch their backs, but Ernie is nuzzled up close to Bert, his head resting on his neck, the way friends do, sometimes. Clearly, given that they're staring at the Supreme Court, and given last week's momentous decision on same-sex marriage, one can only put two and two together and surmise that Bert and Ernie must have a very special reason to be interested.

I smiled immediately. I got it. But then I wondered, until now, who among us guessed that these two lovable puppets might just be gay? I don't know about you, but I grew up without ever giving much thought to another person's sexual orientation (let alone an imaginary character's). It was a simpler world back then, I suppose, or more repressed. Or more stupid, I don't know which. People were pretty much people, characters were characters, puppets, puppets. When I was in college I met a few men who I imagined were more drawn to their own sex than the other, but they never said anything outright. It was all guesswork then; and my conclusions about them hinged on the smallest bits of circumstantial evidence: their obsession with Oscar Wilde or Rock Hudson or their love of ballet, nothing that would ever hold up in court, supreme or otherwise.

Now, thank God, we're largely through with all that. No one seems to care, which is as it should be. And I'm sure that, beyond the joy of the moment, our gay and lesbian brothers and sisters are breathing well deserved sighs of relief. More and more we seem to be okay with the idea of live and let live, and that can't help but be beneficial to everyone.

Oh, I know the battle for tolerance is always ongoing, and we have to be vigilant, and that there are (and always will be) a few odd places in this country where justice gets confused with a particular verse of the Bible, but for now, at least, let's admit we've moved on. Surely that's something we can all smile about.

My Grandma Looms Large in Foreign Policy
March 8, 2014

For some reason, my grandmother and her global adventures keep popping up on my radar lately. Last week I was writing about how fortunate it was for me that in 1907 she didn't change course midstream on her way to America to follow her Polish lover. This week, with Ukraine in the news, I am reminded that my baba hailed from a little berg about one thumbprint west of Kiev on the map, a town near the Dnieper River called Novogradvalensk. Life was pretty tough back then: Of her ten brothers and sisters, she was the only one chosen by the magnanimous Tsar to go to school. Jews were heavily taxed and systematically barred from many professions; even worse, they were the subject of periodic pogroms and other violence by Cossacks and other drunken lowlifes.

She wasn't in the least bit sad to leave the Ukraine. "Russia," she often used to say, "was a great place to be from." That said, one can't help but feel for the plight of the current Ukrainian population who, if one is to believe the Western press, only yearn to live in peace and freedom. And though it's too soon to predict how all this will play out, I'm sure my grandmother—were she still alive—would have recognized another old reliable Cossack in the face of Vladimir Putin.

As a side note, you'd think that our Republican friends in Congress and on television would want to stay as far away from Putin as possible, but no, they seem strangely drawn to him. That's one Russian who knows how to put facts on the ground—that is the general consensus you hear on the right. That's leadership. Now why can't our President Obama act so decisively?

It used to be, as I recall, that when we were confronted with an international crisis, the country pulled together. At the water's edge, there was unanimity. You didn't hear the minority party carping about our government's response when, one Sunday morning the Japanese bombed Pearl Harbor, or not long ago, when nineteen hijackers from the Middle East leveled the World Trade Center. Why is it so different this time?

Republicans demand action, but what, exactly are we supposed to do? Does Senator McCain really want us, for example, to declare war on Russia? I can't imagine. Does Rudy Giuliani believe, in his heart of hearts, that we should funnel weapons into Ukraine? Maybe put some boots on the ground? After more than a decade of conflict and a burnt out military, who now is going to step forward for this craziest of missions? And even if we don't wind up going to war, what good would it do just to rattle our sabers? As Eugene Robinson wrote recently in the newspaper, there are many countries out there that would be intimidated by the sight of an American fleet on the horizon. Russia, however, is not one of them.

What we really need now (and why I'm thankful Obama is President) is for cooler heads to prevail. I don't know about you, but I don't want to go back to the hair-trigger brinksmanship of the Cold War. Nor do I want us to go rushing into situations where we have no earthly idea how it will end. This includes places like Iraq. Also Libya, Syria, and Iran. And now I'd humbly suggest we throw in Russia as well. It may be 2014 and not 1907 anymore, but my grandmother nailed it years ago: it's still a good place to be from.

Ticket to Ride
June 14, 2015

Many, many years ago my mother signed up to take a trip to the moon. No, seriously. She bought a ticket (or what would someday be a ticket) from Pan Am Airlines for the grand price of five or ten dollars, which stated that when commercial traffic to the moon became a reality she could turn that in and hop on board. And she kept that ticket in her sock drawer for a very long time, even after Mr. Armstrong put his foot down on the moon and they planted the flag and played a little golf, all that important stuff astronauts did. And because she was averse to throwing things out, as were many children of the Great Depression, she still had it when Pan Am finally went bankrupt and vanished for good.

I bring this up now because I read an article the other day about a group of Jews in Israel who are raising big money to put a Torah on board a rocket ship and send it to the moon. Not only a Torah, but the Hindu scriptures known as the Veda and, perhaps for luck, a copy of the I Ching. The idea is that these things are sacred, and embody much of the world's moral wisdom, and if they could be kept "safe" on the moon, then if something should happen to the earth, well. By the way, if you are Christian and happen to be reading this, apparently there is already a copy of the New Testament up there somewhere, so not to worry.

I think I understand the primal urge for immortality. I mean, I don't particularly want to live forever, but I can see how some folks might want to have their life story put on a perpetual film loop and shown to their descendants. I even kind of get the impulse of people who want to be cryogenically frozen so they can come back in two hundred years (when of course science has cured all diseases) and wake up with the energy of a nine-year old. Nothing wrong with that, I suppose.

But it seems to me something is whacked with this Torah-on-the-moon notion: For one thing, if we're going to use the moon as a storage space, as another cloud technology, doesn't that suggest we have little or no faith that the earth will endure? And if we believe the whole world is going to hell in a handbasket, that total destruction is inevitable, how can we be sure when Armageddon comes, that the moon will somehow be spared? More to the point, isn't the crux of the Torah to be found in living an ethical life here on Earth? And if we can't keep the Earth from disintegrating, the fact that there is this ancient grand plan for living a sweet life on Earth, but—drat—it's sitting in a hermetically sealed capsule on the moon, well, that's rather awkward, isn't it.

Jews have always placed great value upon words, maybe because for much of our existence, we had precious little else. But this seems—you'll forgive me—like a bridge to nowhere. Now maybe if there were a synagogue up there, Temple Beth Luna, a decent rabbi, a cantor with a voice that didn't make people want to stand up and leave, well, that might be different. You'd need a Torah then, on a dark, cold Friday night. And folks like my mother, who kept their Pan Am tickets faithfully.

Let's Talk it Over
April 20, 2013

Whether or not the fellow (and it is surely a fellow) who planted those bombs in Boston hails from the Middle East or Middletown, USA, one thing is abundantly clear: we are no longer protected by oceans on either side. No, we are now part of a contentious, and increasingly violent global neighborhood. People, from the Taliban to the Teapartiers, all have their own demands and opinions, and it is no longer the case that folks can agree to disagree, much less compromise.

I frankly don't understand why compromise has gotten such a bum rap lately. Almost every bit of deal making in business is just compromise, after all, bending and remolding a square peg to fit it into a round hole, taking fifty rupees less for your "priceless" heirloom. If business can compromise regularly, why can't our political leaders? And this is all the more galling when you realize that most of our political leaders—if not owned outright—at least take most of their marching orders from business.

I know that what businessmen and businesswomen care about above all is making money, I get that, but when they come home at night and kick off their shoes and unwind their ties, they are also human beings, aren't they? What do I mean by "human"? Well, something simple, for example: they have children that they'd like to see get through the whole school day without getting shot. Or they have friends and relatives who run marathons. Or they have gay brothers and sisters who they know deserve to be treated equally under the law. And here in California, they probably have considerable day-to-day contact with undocumented workers, people who don't always speak English—gardeners and house-cleaners and cooks and nannies without whom life would be anything but easy.

That's the America I see, anyway. All these people, good and not so good, rich and poor, working together, compromising, making deals and temporary arrangements so they can get through another day, another week. Practical people trying as best they can to solve one another's problems. But somehow on the political level, this process of talking rationally and brainstorming and compromising doesn't happen. What happens instead is the madness of what occurred on the streets of Boston the other day.

We Do What We Do
September 2012

Many people think that because we're in the book business, there is some grand plan involved in what we do. Books presuppose wisdom and culture and civilized behavior, after all, and you can't have any of those things without careful preparation.

Well, let me disabuse you of that notion. Lilla and I got into the book trade because we were seduced by a dream. Once upon a time, Matthew, our friend in the Berkshires, had a bookshop (still does) that we adored and were envious of (even though it was clear he wasn't making two plug nickels at it). We both had somewhat boring jobs that translated into somewhat decent salaries, and we thought, in the way that salaried people who spend inordinate amounts of time browsing in bookstores do, that maybe somehow, someday, we could do this, too. It was an idle wish, not unlike the kind you make when you close your eyes and blow out your birthday candles. But soon we saw that this was a crazy idea. We couldn't start another bookstore in the Berkshires when Matthew was hanging on by his fingernails; that way we'd probably both go broke. And worse still, it would be the kiss of death to our friendship.

Around this time Lilla made one of her periodic homesick jaunts back to California to see our family. As luck would have it, she was walking around the plaza when she noticed there wasn't a New England style literary bookshop here in Sonoma. Oh, she said. (Actually, I don't know what she said. I'm just paraphrasing her Eureka! moment.)

That's the short version of how we came to be here. There was no thinking, really. There was just a romantic yearning coupled with an empty storefront for rent on East Napa Street. That's not chopped liver, of course. Many sweet, chubby, little babies are conceived out of far less material. But it's also not planned.

Which leads me to my big, startling idea: I believe that the best songs, the best shoes, the best pizza, the best businesses, in short, the best of everything out there, have almost nothing whatsoever to do with planning. Oh, we plan and we practice. That's good. But what really drives success is a bit of luck and a whole lot of passion—love of winemaking, love of joke-telling, love of people and deal-making. Without love and luck and hands-on creativity, all you're left with in the end is a room filled with stuff. An air-conditioned nightmare, as Henry Miller used to say. We've all been in deadly places like that, those well-planned barns where the staff is bored to tears but still try to look busy while slyly waiting for five o'clock to roll around.

That's not what we do here. No, we're in love. We're smitten with books and stories and the magic of words. And I'll take that anytime over two plug nickels.

Public and Private Reflections
September 2007

If you read the local paper you may have chanced upon the article back in August about Readers' Books being named the 2007 Business of the Year by the Chamber of Commerce. This is, of course, a big honor, and I would be a callous and loathsome creature if I did not accept everyone's praise with the grace and humility for which I am known around the world. I hear there is also a fancy luncheon involved, and perhaps a plaque of some kind. This is great stuff, no doubt, a feather in our cap, especially when you realize that up until now Business of the Year (BOTY) has been pretty much the exclusive domain of the Big Guys—banks, supermarkets, raceways. Not to take anything away from them—a BOTY is a BOTY, after all. They give away cars, donate blood, raise money, cure cancer. They do good works and the community appreciates them for it. That's the usual definition of a BOTY.

But Readers' Books is tiny by comparison, a seat-of-the-pants operation if there ever was one. We had no business plan when we started, no mission statement, no demographic study. In fact, if we'd gone to the trouble to develop a plan and actually considered all the risks, I'm quite sure we never would have opened our doors at all. Right now we have maybe eight or ten employees, depending on how you count, and none of us are getting rich. It's always difficult to park around here, the air-conditioning works when it chooses, our computers have minds of their own, and, even after 15 years, the cost and worry of running a business still keeps us up late into the night. We are and will always be the Little Guy—the Marx Brothers vs. the Establishment, David vs. Goliath.

Sure, okay, we also do good works. Admittedly, we've brought hundreds, maybe thousands of authors to Sonoma over the years, and I'd like to think that the community's spirit and intellect is better for it. This is not the same as curing cancer, of course, but I'll take what I can get.

To tell you the truth, the first person I thought of when I heard that we were BOTY was my father. He never won any awards that I know of. He would be 92 years old about now and right up to the very end he loved working at the bookstore. It was the "best medicine," he always said. It gave him a reason to get up in the morning. My dad would have been proud of us, I imagine. He wasn't much for grand displays of emotion, but he would have smiled or patted us quietly on the back or given us a "thumbs up" sign when he thought no one was looking. That's something I would give my right arm for, even now.

What Einstein Might Have Missed
April 21, 2012

Don't know why, but somehow I find myself operating at warp speed these days. This morning I was rushing all around, unable to find my toothbrush, my wristwatch, and then, when I finally climbed in and sat behind the wheel of the car, my keys. Not a good way to start the day. This in turn reminded me of an old New Yorker cartoon: Albert Einstein has come to the end of a whole series of complex equations on the blackboard, wherein he discovers to his amazement that, in fact, time equals money.

My time in the bookstore, sadly, does not equal money. At least not a lot of money. It's okay. I have accepted this notion, that money does not come with the territory. You take the good with the bad—what other choice do you have? A plumber or an electrician must realize sooner or later that crawling around in the presence of muck and rats and cobwebs comes with the territory. And mailmen develop problems with their backs and knees. You walk along in the sun with a heavy sack on your shoulder for twenty years, and guess what?—it happens.

Occasionally I wish I had a career which included vast amounts of money. I imagine I would give great gobs of it away to people who really need it. Poor people, orphans, the homeless. I imagine funding some scientific group working on a cancer cure or a new solar car. We booksellers do get to dream, thank you very much, and while it's hard to cash those dreams at the bank, it's also true that sometimes the things you care most about are the things you can't put a price on. I can live with that, too.

Of Giraffes, Snow, and Lolita
September 2005

Among the many fun perks we enjoy here at Readers' Books is the daily opportunity to match wits with those of our customers. It looks like this: a man will wander in and say, "I was just driving in my car and caught the tailend of an interview with some guy on NPR who wrote a book. I didn't catch his name. Steve something. Or maybe Phil, I dunno. You have it?"

At this point it is my turn to bounce the ball. I say, "Did you happen to hear the title?" Or, "Can you remember even one word from the title? They usually state it right after the interview."

"Nah, I was busy driving, see? My mind was on the road. But wait, wait! It was something about wild animals. Hyenas or elephants. Yeah, that's it. And the guy sounded a lot like a Brit or an Irishman."

Now this is far more information than we ordinarily get. I make a careful review of the clues. NPR. Steve or Phil. Wild animal in the title. British or Irish author. Granted, intelligence of this sort is murky, as our government officials are constantly reminding us. An art, not a science. Still, I feel something bubbling up inside of me, a profile of our culprit. "Does he—this Steve or Phil—have other books to his name? Is this a series, do you suppose?"

"Could be," he says.

Now, I think, that clinches it. I will be bold and venture forth with a guess. "Is it Alexander McCall Smith? His second book—*Tears of the Giraffe*?"

"Yes!" my startled customer shouts. "How on earth did you know?"

The truth is, I don't know how I know. It's intuitive, or maybe sometimes counter-intuitive, all depending.

Once someone came in and the only clue to the book they offered was that it was "a mystery with a lot of S's in the title." Without blinking an eye I said, "*Smilla's Sense of Snow*." How did I know? Because after years of playing Stump the Bookseller, you reach a point when the fog suddenly evaporates and seven times out of ten, you get it right. Some people call this genius; others say dumb luck. I'd prefer to think of it rather as a result of the constant practice we do here to familiarize ourselves with our books. We check them in, we shelve them, we sell them, we return them. We even occasionally read them.

But that doesn't mean we can find them. For instance, if somebody comes in and says they saw a book at your store a month ago and all they know is that it had a blue cover, I'd probably give up right away. First, because if that's all they remember, you could be hunting for it from now until next summer. Second, because if they couldn't be bothered to buy it then there is no reason to think they'd buy it now. Third, (and this is most important) it probably wasn't a blue cover anyway.

Then there are those who know the book (approximately) but their description seems to launch you into a different dimension altogether. For example, we sell a very popular book called *Reading Lolita in Tehran*—a memoir of an Iranian woman's teaching experience under the fundamentalist regime. Three weeks ago woman came in and she wanted a copy of Reading Lolita in "Hanoi." Okay, Tehran, Hanoi, we can adjust. Then two nights ago another woman came in and asked for Reading Lolita in "Iraq." Suddenly my hair was on fire. Is this a trend? Does it speak to our run amok fear of terrorism? A new strain of mental illness? Literary multilateralism? What? Or maybe just another example of America's let's-go-slow approach to learning geography. Hmmm.

One can overthink these things, to be sure. But then that's another perk of bookselling.

The Best(seller) Years of Our Lives
May 2006

A word or two about bestsellers. You may have noticed that virtually every book published nowadays is a bestseller or penned by the bestselling author of something-or-other, or destined to be a bestseller. If you are a discerning person—that is, the kind of person for whom words still have meaning—you are probably alarmed. People should not be allowed to fling terms like bestseller around willy-nilly, after all. It is confusing at best, and disingenuous at worst.

But wait, there's more. Once you open up the can of worms that is bestsellerdom all kinds of oddities emerge. There are questions. For example, how does one determine a bestseller, anyway? You'd imagine it'd be simple, no? Just check what has been sold at bookstores week after week and whoever comes out on top wins. If that's what you imagined, you imagined wrong. Take that bastion of authenticity, The New York Times. They don't reveal their methodology, but not long ago the talk in the business was that they didn't go solely by books sold, but also by books purchased by large wholesalers and big box stores. In other words, if Superstore X bought a half million copies of a book, it was, overnight as it were, a bestseller. There is a certain interior faith-based logic to this. After all, why would a buyer go out on a limb and order that many copies if he or she didn't sincerely believe it was going to be a huge hit? You might also ask why some people persist in seeing the image of Jesus in an oil slick, for that matter. And to err is human. But what if the buyer made a mistake? What if the book was a dud? Not to worry. Launching it prematurely onto a national bestseller list guarantees a respectable number of sales anyway—voila! A bestseller is born.

Like I say, they may not do this sort of thing now, they may be honorable and well-meaning and all that, but if you look at the Times bestseller list you have to wonder. For instance, looking at last week's list, only 5 of the 16 books on the hardcover fiction list have sold at Readers' Books. Our best sellers—*A Thousand Years of Good Prayers, Brief History of the Dead*, and even *The March*—are nowhere to be seen.

There are far more reliable bestseller lists, fortunately. The Book Sense list is an accurate reflection of books sold by independent bookstores nationwide. They ask us what we've sold, and, by God, we tell them. What's interesting about Book Sense is that people read different books in different parts of the United States. Turns out, Harold Brodky has only a little following in Northern California and you can hardly give Ken Kesey away in New York. Book Sense has both a regional bestseller list and a national bestseller list. But even so, both lists closely reflect the books that actually sell at Readers'. The other lists have got us scarfing up Danielle Steel and Robert Ludlum by the pound. I hope they're wrong. Gosh, I hope they're wrong.

A Death in the Family
September 12, 2011

Sometime around the middle of October, my friends Jeff and Jennifer, who own Sonoma Bookends, will close their doors for the last time. I understand why they're doing it; just about everyone in retail weighs that option on a regular basis. In the end, though, most of us shrug and go back to work, we soldier on, not because it's making us much money; it's really more because we care so dearly about what we do. If you were just looking at numbers, you might say that that's the definition of insanity, and nobody would argue with you. Still, the notion of them being gone and Readers' being the last bookstore in town feels bad, like a death in the family.

When I spoke with him the other day, Jeff pointed out that at the moment, Nashville, Tennessee, a city far larger than Sonoma, has no bookstore. Zero. Nada. This will be remedied soon by the author Ann Patchett, who lives there and plans to open one. That's nice. Ann Patchett is a wonderful writer, and God knows she has more than enough money to float something like that. But the larger point is that tiny Sonoma has somehow sustained two bookstores over the course of twenty years, and it may well be that people don't realize what a streak of luck this has been.

I run a bookstore, which is a delicate balancing act. But the real questions I keep coming back to are much deeper than economics. What do we value? What kind of world do we want our children to live in? Does it mean anything that we call ourselves civilized? For myself, I simply wouldn't live in a town that did not support a decent bookstore, a forum for writers and new ideas. I wouldn't live in a town that didn't have a fine theater like the Sebastiani, where kids are encouraged to get up on stage and express themselves, or a pub like Murphy's, that brings in local musicians.

Jeff said he hopes we get a bounce out of this, that some of his customers will no doubt drift over to us. Maybe so. Jeff's not insane; he's chosen to move on. But in my heart I would much rather see him stay. It's not about the money. It's about each other.

Why Borders Matters, Why Everything Matters
August 5, 2011

When the mega-bookstore chain, Borders, liquidated their last seven hundred stores, it did not go unnoticed at Readers' Books. Several customers commented hopefully that now that we were rid of "that awful chain store," our business would perk up (it hasn't yet) or, at the very least, that we should feel good that we are still standing while Borders has bitten the proverbial dust. We must be doing something right, after all, to have outlasted them.

The truth is far more nuanced, however. For one thing, we were never really in competition with Borders. They never located in the town of Sonoma where the bulk of our customers live. They may have been a problem for Copperfield's in Santa Rosa, but even that is something I have no first-hand knowledge of. What strikes me most about Borders closing is how much we are losing. Not the books, the books that Borders sold will still be available in stores like ours. No, what's disappearing is human capital. Some 11,000 people are being let go across the country, people who read and considered and sold books to millions of Americans. These people were experts in their way; they filtered information, they knew exactly what their customers wanted, and were always on the look-out for new titles to satisfy an untold number of needs and desires. They were the connection—the missing link— between the constantly changing printed universe and their hungry fan base. And now they are gone. This is not a population that is easily replaced. You cannot go on Amazon and find a community of knowledgeable people to help you choose a great read. Amazon can tell you what other people have read and liked, but that's like being lost in a strange city and asking a perfect stranger where to eat. It's shooting in the dark.

The truth is I feel sad when any bookstore closes, because it makes it just that much harder to live a life with grace and wit and civility. And what are we here for, after all, beyond eating and sleeping and making more of us? That's why Borders matters. That's why everything matters.

Research and I Have the Facts at my Fingertips
June 28, 2014

When we got into this business back in 1991, we looked at the people who came through the door and determined, through a clever use of science and magical thinking, that our customer base was approximately 75% local and 25% tourist. How did we do this, exactly? Well, first we became savvy readers of people. Also, we conducted random surveys. We would look at someone we didn't recognize (which was everyone, initially) and ask, "So....where abouts are ya from?" And if they said Sonoma or Glen Ellen, or even Kenwood, we'd nod sagely, then, when they weren't looking, we'd put a hash mark down in the LOCAL column. And, if somebody came in as pale as a ghost and speaking with a heavy Boston twang, or tanned but wearing pink shorts and an LA Dodger cap, or well dressed, but murmuring in German or Russian or Hebrew, we might not ask them that question, in fact, we might not ask them anything at all, but we'd for sure put them down as TOURIST. Then, after many months of this thankless work, we'd add up our numbers and—lo and behold—it was 75 to 25.

Now, I'm here to report that that mix has undergone a seismic shift: about 25% of our customers come from the Valley of the Moon, while the rest (that would be 75%) are from out of the area. Let's leave aside whether this is absolutely true or whether I'm just imagining it for a moment. I mean, I know the scientific reasoning which led me to my first set of conclusions is, admittedly, suspect and perhaps even sophomoric, but let's take a deep breath and pretend I'm right, that it's a fact. How and why did this come about? That's the real question.

Here's what I think: In the first place, a number of our old time customers have either moved away, gotten infirm, or, sadly, died. I know this for a fact, and it's a natural process, after all. People get old, stop reading, die. In the second place, the young people here, maybe because there are not enough good jobs in Sonoma, or because they get bored silly with small town life, or because it's in their DNA to see whether the grass is greener in New York or Paris, leave. I've seen this with my own eyes. Lastly, it must be stated that the City Council and the wineries and the Chamber of Commerce and the Visitors Bureau and others have done a bang-up job promoting tiny little Sonoma as the town that time forgot. That's why the sidewalk around the Plaza seems so crowded these days: it's our own doing; we have deliberately opened the door to folks who used to live in quaint places like ours, but can't quite remember when.

As the owner of the last bookstore in town, I have to say that I don't mind this new trend nearly as much as perhaps some others do. Tourists help pay our bills, and their money is still green (actually, that's kind of changing, too, but never mind). And we still have many, many loyal customers who aren't bored or sick or dead yet, people who aren't afraid to come in regularly and joke around like in the olden days, which is something we cherish. And business has actually started to improve. Along with many other shops, we're gradually coming back from the Dreaded Recession. You may have noticed, for example, that we put down a new carpet (the old one was so shabby it was getting ready to walk away on its own). This is a good thing. We paid Rugworks, a friendly, local company, a nice chunk of money and they did a marvelous job. The guy who contracted the job came in later and bought some books from us, probably using some of the cash we gave him. That's the way it should work.

The only thing we need to guard against now is this death thing. We just have to stay healthy. I mean, if all the locals die out, there'll be nothing but tourists here. And tourists never die. That's a fact.

On Chasing Rainbows
November 2011

My Uncle Bernie married my Aunt Elsie on a dare. They had three children together and a complicated, noisy, and altogether miserable marriage, which was exacerbated by the fact that it went on forever. Truth was, they hated each other, but, in those days, no one they knew ever considered divorce. It simply wasn't done.

I bring this familial tidbit up because we are about to embark on our twentieth anniversary at Readers' Books, which, as it happens, was also begun whimsically. We were living in Western Massachusetts in 1990, and Lilla came back from visiting my brother and his family in Sonoma. We were fine where we were, the kids were happy, the grass was green, but we were a tad restless.

"You know what we ought to do?" she said one evening. "We should just quit our jobs and sell everything and move back to California. I'll bet they could use a good old fashioned New England style literary bookstore in Sonoma." (Full disclosure: we had fantasized once about starting a bookstore in the Berkshires, but that would entail going into competition with our best friend, who was already hanging on by his fingernails.)

My response to this was quick and to the point: "Okay," I said.

Now some couples (most couples, probably) have conversations like this and they go nowhere. We, however, put our house on the market the next day. And two days later, we had an offer. The rest, as they say, is history.

On their 40th wedding anniversary, their children gave my aunt and uncle a dinner party in one of those bar mitzvah palaces that New Yorkers rent out for such occasions. They assembled all their old, still vertical friends from years past, they catered it, hired a band, did their best to make it festive. The family was seated at a long white table on stage facing the audience. No one spoke. Finally, their diplomatic and ever hopeful daughter-in-law raised a glass of champagne. "Well," she said, "here's to the next forty years."

To which my Aunt Elsie replied bluntly: "You've got to be kidding."

All of which brings me back to our own anniversary. Let me just say that Lilla and I have had a fabulous time here with you. Let me also add that we don't hate each other, or you, or anyone really (well, I'm not so fond of Amazon). Moreover, we—and by "we," I mean not just me and Lilla, but every one of our staff who've helped turn Readers' Books into the charming, quirky outpost it is—we're glad we made that lightning decision in 1990.

As my late Uncle Bernie might say, sometimes your instincts can lead you astray. What I know is this, however: life is short, and sometimes you just have to act on your instincts. Otherwise, you'll never get to see how beautiful it is on the other side of the rainbow. So thanks, everyone. And here's to the next twenty years.

Idle Pleasures
January 2005

When I was nine or ten, I was an obsessive reader of Sherlock Holmes, and, in my teenage years, I admit I even briefly entertained the notion of becoming a detective. That is, until I read Studs Terkel's account of what private investigators actually do—i.e., pour over old musty files in government buildings or, worse, follow people around, usually husbands or wives, to see if they're cheating on their spouses, which means spending hours and hours in a parked car eating junk food, waiting for something (anything) to happen. This seemed to my disappointed young mind then (and to my jaded older mind now) a supremely boring way to waste one's life.

As a bookseller, however, I can still pretend to be Sherlock Holmes. This is because I'm blessed with customers who periodically bring in boxes and bags of old books to recycle—books they may have read but no longer want, books they found in their dead Aunt Edna's attic, books their ex-boyfriend left behind when he moved out. It is my task (some would preface that with "thankless") to go through those books, to parse them and form them into succinct piles—yes, no, maybe. I've gotten pretty good at this operation—well, maybe not good, but fast. What I choose often boils down to condition vs. title. Do I, for example, take this copy of *On the Road*, a great book and easy to resell, when it has clearly been read nearly to death, the spine bent, the margins filled with scholarly comments like "awk!" and "derivative!" and "what does this mean?" Alas, Watson, I cannot. Or do I accept this gently read, almost new copy of *Waiting for Godot?* Again, I must decline. Beckett's play is terrific, of course, but no one has asked for it in the last ten years and besides I already have three copies on the shelf. There are reasons people are divesting themselves of these books, in other words, and book sleuths like me know them all too well. One must be careful.

You can glean a lot, though, just sifting through another person's books. How they grew up, what they dreamt once of becoming, where they used to live, what languages they learned, how their relationships may have faltered along the way, illnesses, etc. And then there are always the unexplained, anecdotal things, things they used as bookmarks. A photograph of a nameless prepubescent girl in a sunny backyard demonstrating her skill with a hula hoop, a Nutcracker ballet program from thirty years ago, a baggage tag for a flight to Paris, a love letter, and once, even, a summons from Highway Patrol. There are snapshots of family vacations in Tahoe, favorite dogs in silly costumes, distant relatives, or maybe they are perfect strangers, holding hands on board some ocean liner. Hard to tell.

Wherever we go, we leave our fingerprints behind like amateur car thieves. And it is my idle pleasure to speculate about this or that clue, to piece it together with whatever else I know. Sometimes I solve little mysteries this way. Sometimes I am led astray. It doesn't matter really. And it sure beats sitting around in parked cars eating junk food.

More from the Secret Lives of Booksellers
July 2013

People are forever coming up to the counter with a book in their hands and asking me if I've read it. Let me tell you, nine times out of ten the answer is no, and not for the reasons you might think. You might think, for example, that I hadn't read it because I don't like that particular author, or because I don't read sports stories or science fiction or books that take place out doors. (Actually, it's sort of true, I don't much care for books that are set out doors, I mean, all those bugs and mangy critters, not to mention the heat, the cold, the tornadoes, just the overall cruelty and unpredictability of Mother Nature, who needs it?) No, the real reason I haven't read that book you're holding hopefully in your hands (and it may be a perfectly wonderful book) is that there are just too many books in my world.

You see, while we in the bookselling community often walk around clothed in a style that can best be called "Early Refugee" and do not bring home huge pay checks or go on extravagant trips to Paris, we do nevertheless enjoy some perks. One of them is that we get to read advanced reading copies of many things. Publishers send us these galleys, not because they feel sorry for us or because they love us—no, they want us to read them and order them in huge quantities and sell them to you. It's like the free bite of fruit or cheese you may have tried at Whole Foods; they want something from you, but you don't really have to comply.

So, in a similar manner, we receive these promo books that won't hit the market for months and months. When you ask what we're reading at the moment, that's it. They are books you can't buy because they don't exist. Not for you, anyway, not technically. And every season, there are hundreds of them. Which is great fun if you love books. It's like being a kid in a candy store, but there are only so many hours in a day and one can only read so much. We pick and choose, therefore, and many worthy books go unread. If, at this point you're thinking, hey, that's not an efficient way to run things, you're right, but nobody ever accused publishers of being efficient. In the big scheme of things, they're actually much more akin to salmon; some of their eggs turn into fish and swim out to sea, but many, oh so many, don't.

What usually happens is that someone here will read a book and fall in love with it, and then start selling it, one copy at a time. That love gets passed around from person to person until a tipping point is reached and then suddenly, the author is doing interviews on the Today Show. Think *Angela's Ashes* or *House of Sand and Fog* or *The Glass Castle*. I can name dozens of books that went to the moon like that, books that might have died quiet deaths if a few independent booksellers hadn't picked them up early on and gone to bat for them.

It's not fair, of course. That book you're holding in your hands is probably worth its weight in gold; I'm sure the author poured his heart and soul into it, but what am I going to do? I'm just one person, with one set of slowly failing eyes. So the truth is, it's up to you, dear reader. You have the power. You have to make that leap of faith. You have to buy that book and sit down and read it. And then, if you want to do me a real favor, tell me if it was any good.

The Question
September 2006

When my dad was 84, he had one of his knees replaced. Actually, he should have had both knees done, but since he was a cautious man by nature, he wanted to try things out one at a time. The procedure went smoothly, but the recovery took six months, and as my father told me many times, it was painful. As a result, he swore off knee surgery forever and limped through the remainder of his life. His doctors never explained to him about the pain involved. They talked about "procedures" (not shocking surgical operations). They talked about "pain management" (whatever that is). It wasn't their knee, after all.

I bring this up in order to offer a few words about the bookstore, and a question that is asked of us here at least once a month: When are you going to start serving coffee? As if bookstores just naturally serve coffee along with jokes and magazines. It is always asked in a well-meaning manner, and of course there is an inner logic to it: people like coffee and books. They "go" together in the way say that hotdogs go with baseball. Other (unmentionable) bookstores have started serving coffee and it has proven to be a money-making idea. And independent bookstores are struggling these days, it's true. So why not.

Well, we've thought about it. We even talked with people in the coffee business about the feasibility. And in the end we decided that to make room for coffee we'd have to jettison a sizeable portion of the bookstore, which is a bit like cutting off one's nose (I keep coming back to surgery for some reason) to spite one's face. Besides, we thought, there are at least six pretty good coffee establishments within a stone's throw of Readers' Books. Many of these folks are our friends. Can we or should we compete with them? Where do we draw the line?

Sometimes a good idea is only good in abstract. If we had a vast amount of space, and if there wasn't another drop of coffee to be had in town, maybe then it would make sense.

We welcome everyone's ideas, of course. We're all about ideas. But when you've started something from scratch and nurtured it patiently along for fifteen years, something happens to your point of view. In the end, I guess, this is our bookstore, our knee. My father would have understood.

What You Is & What You Ain't
April 26, 2014

It is both disappointing and troubling to hear that Philip Roth has decided to retire from the business of writing. I mean, okay, he's going on eighty years old, and if he has nothing further to say, well then, he should just quit writing. But that is qualitatively different than retiring. A plumber retires, or a certified public accountant, or an engineer. Those folks have carved out a little niche. They've gone to school, gotten a degree and a certain proficiency in whatever. They've put in their time and then, when they turn sixty-five, they're ready for the ritual of retirement: the gold watch, the certificate of appreciation, the pat on the back, and they're gone. They may have liked what they did in their working days well enough, but now what they would really prefer to do is watch baseball or golf or, I don't know, volunteer for Meals on Wheels or putter in the garden. Nothing wrong with any of that, and I'm not casting aspersions on plumbers or engineers. They are, generally speaking, normal people, and that's the normal pattern of retirement.

A writer, however, is, like a musician or a painter—not normal. A writer is a person utterly given over to his or her passion; passion is the battery that drives them, it's the reason they get up every morning, which is just another fancy way of saying that writing makes them insanely happy. I know this personally because writing and playing the guitar make me insanely happy. In fact, while I don't mind doing the dishes or selling books or paying publishers, I would much rather be writing or playing the guitar than any other activity. (Note: I include sex here, too, although sex is fun, if I remember correctly). Am I crazy? Maybe. But that's the landscape artists inhabit. There's nothing to be done about it.

Which brings me back to Philip Roth. He has written some remarkable novels in his life, stories that should have earned him a Nobel Prize, stories that— for me, at least—have done wonders to illuminate not only his Newark, New Jersey, angst-riddled Jewish ghetto, but my own universe as well. I haven't read everything he's written, I admit, and there were a few of his earlier novels which, while best-sellers at the time, felt juvenile and half-baked. To his credit, though, he didn't give up; his writing matured, he worked tirelessly, and it shows: so many of the books he's written over the years—*The Counterlife, American Pastoral, The Plot Against America, The Ghost Writer, Indignation, Nemesis,* to name a few—have been gems. And to this day I can still remember scenes from them and the feelings they evoked.

If he's weary now and just wants to spend his last days visiting art museums in Manhattan and having lunch with friends, I'm fine with that. But if he cares at all about how he's lived his life and the great cultural mother lode he's produced, well, then, he shouldn't say he's retiring. Writers don't retire. They stop writing. Musicians don't retire. They don't gig anymore. But they're still writers, they're still musicians. It's in the blood. You don't walk away from who you are.

The Luck of the Draw
May 2013

It was John Updike, I believe, who said that whenever he sits down to write a novel, he isn't thinking about the metropolitan crowds who will hear about it on the Today Show and immediately rush out and snatch it off the display table in some glitzy bookstore. No, his ideal customer is quite different. He pictures a young, earnest person in a small town in the middle of Iowa maybe, someone who has a few extra minutes to kill and wanders into a public library, someone who is just browsing the stacks aimlessly when all at once he comes upon that book. The title makes him stop. It's familiar or it reminds him of a conversation he once had with an old friend or with a long lost love. Something resonates inside this person and he (or she) pulls it off the shelf and turns to the first page.

Many of my most pleasurable adventures in life have happened that way. I wasn't looking for a particular title. My mind was elsewhere. It was almost as if the book I really needed to read at that moment (*Steppenwolf, The Loved One, A Hundred Camels in the Courtyard, The Day of the Locust*) just sidled up out of nowhere and wedged itself into my hands by magic.

I say "almost" because I am not, by disposition, a proponent of magic. Even though I got a D in high school chemistry and don't ever really care to know what goes on under the hood of a car, when push comes to shove, I'll still put my money down on science every time. Full disclosure: my younger son is a magician, and, yes, of course, that sort of thing—sleight of hand, misdirection, logical trickery—is fascinating and endlessly entertaining.

That said, I can't help but feel a little residual fluttering in my fingertips whenever I land upon that certain book I didn't realize I was longing for all my life. And I thank my lucky stars (not that I have any) because here I was, in the right place at the right time, blessed, you might say, if you believed in God (not really) and shazam!—Just like that, I'm reading this dynamite book. Is this a great country or what?

A Year to Remember
January 2009

A trend is afoot. We suddenly have an endless stream of titles that denote a pivotal year in history. There is *1491* (the year before Columbus came and decimated all those peace-loving American Indians) and *1421* (when the Chinese discovered us and promptly disappeared). There's June, *1941* (the year Hitler ran wild over Europe and things looked, well, bad) and *1942* (just a bad year generally) and *1968* (when America came unhinged over sex, drugs, and Vietnam). Oh yes, and let's don't forget *1453* (when the Turkish navy was defeated, which meant they'd never again bother those peace-loving Europeans) and predictive texts like *2012* (when the Mayans and others who smoke ayahuasca sincerely believe in the coming of a big paradigm shift, whatever that is).

All of which brings me to 2008. There is no book out yet, but there surely will be, and I'd like get the jump on anyone contemplating such a project. With the exception of Barack Obama's electoral victory (no small thing, granted), you'd have to admit it was a pretty miserable year. The stock market plunged, business evaporated, gas prices skyrocketed, hurricanes hit us from all sides, and people (actual people I know) lost their jobs, homes, and marriages. More than a few friends and acquaintances died in 2008, but it's hard to say whether that's because I've simply reached an age when people I know die or because people are always dying and I just happen to know far too many of them.

Still, I have to say I am grateful. The larger truth is that, despite everything, so far we've managed to survive this storm. And when you think about it, we are blessed to be part of a momentous time in history. Sure, everyone is broke right now and the pain is so widespread that only bankruptcy lawyers are immune. We're down, but that doesn't mean we are out. I am grateful for the idea of compassionate change that our new President offers, and for the chance to use our brains again after so many years of blind faith, hand ringing and irrational action. Most of all, I am grateful for the big-hearted resilience of the American people, a character trait we seldom show the rest of the world.

Whoever writes the book on 2008 will have to take note of all these things. Yes, it was a year of fear and near fatal cataclysm. But it may also turn out to be the year we finally came to our senses.

Progress Used to Be Our Most Important Product
March 13, 2013

We have just learned that Rin's Thai Restaurant, a long-time staple of our charming East Napa Street neighborhood, is going to disappear and be replaced by a wine tasting establishment. I should say, yet another wine tasting establishment. If you have wandered around the Plaza lately you are probably familiar with them: I mean, how can you not be? They are everywhere.

Now, as a matter of full disclosure: I have many wonderful friends in the wine world, I drink wine occasionally, I have nothing whatsoever against wine bars in general, and I know that Sonoma is becoming more and more famous for its vintages and watering holes and "the good life," whatever that means.

When we moved to Sonoma, I can assure you it was not on account of the wine bars. Sonoma was still a quaint town then, with history and natural beauty and a worthy literary heritage. Yes, wine was a big element of the area, but not the only one. We came for the whole experience, and it would be my wish that all who come here now also embrace that idea.

I guess the word I'm looking for is balance. When I was eighteen (a lifetime ago), I remember visiting my grandmother, who was living in a suburb of Tel Aviv, a town called Bnei Barak. I knew it was a somewhat devout community, but I was shocked to see that there were not one, but three separate yeshivas (religious schools) on the same block. You had to look hard to find a grocery store. Since then, Bnei Barak has only grown more devout, and it's no longer a place that secular tourists are drawn to. Okay, you could maybe argue that because it's Israel, there's an inherent craziness to how things happen, and I wouldn't necessarily disagree, but does a small town like ours really need 20 wine bars all within a stone's throw of each other? Does this make sense? I know Mae West used to wink and say "too much of a good thing is wonderful" but really, folks, are we not in danger of going just a tad overboard, like Bnei Barak?

In the End, It's All Soup
August 2, 2014

It may be a generalization, but in my experience you don't learn much of anything by going to a wedding. Weddings nowadays are drunken, decorative (overly decorative if you ask me) affairs where people spend far too much money, and they're still smiling, long after the band has packed up and left the stage. This wasn't true many years ago when my cousin Bennett got married, I remember: the bride wasn't Jewish, that was the problem, and Bennett's mother wasn't about to be diplomatic and attend. On top of that, when Bennett tried to crush the wine glass at the end of the ceremony, the damn thing wouldn't break. Not right away, anyway, and I'm sure there were those in the audience who regarded this as a sure sign of tragic things to come. (They're still happily married, by the way, and Bennett's mom has passed away, which just proves my point: wedding superstitions don't matter.)

Funerals, on the other hand, bring out the truth—or lots of different truths—in spades. People speak glowingly of the deceased; they tell little stories that illustrate this or that point. How Ralph was an avid butterfly collector, how funny Helen was at cocktail parties, especially after she'd had a few highballs herself, how devoted Margaret was to all children everywhere, even though her own children kept their distance once they were grown. One of the great advantages of talking about the dead is that they can't talk back. Your version of events—no matter what axe you may still have to grind—that's the truth. In fact, whatever you say becomes part of the canon.

When I rose to speak at my father's funeral, I'm sure I said a few things that were outwardly true. In his youth he was a socialist. Unions and strikes and the Sacco and Vanzetti trial were part of his upbringing, just as the Kennedy assassination and Vietnam were part of mine. He read Karl Marx and he saw suffering and inequality all around him. Given those circumstances, I would be surprised if he hadn't been a socialist. Then Stalin made a pact with Hitler and the war came along and everything changed. He came home looking for opportunity, and by the grace of the GI Bill, he found it. He graduated from pharmacy school, moved to California, bought a tract house, and started reading the Wall Street Journal. He wanted to succeed. It's not that he wanted to fail when he called himself a socialist; perhaps what changed was the definition of success.

As our family made arrangements for his funeral, we realized that flowers were not a big part of my dad's life. I can't recall a single time he ever bought my mother flowers (to be fair, my mother didn't appreciate flowers, either), so on his casket we placed a large colorful basket of root vegetables. These would later be boiled in a pot and made into good, thick, proletarian soup. Looking back now, I don't know that my father would have approved or frowned on this kind of business; it was a metaphor for his life we were aiming at, that's all, a simple, loving way to sum things up. He did like to eat. He once was a socialist. If he had any taste at all, it was probably utilitarian. So okay then, soup. There you go.

Whatever
October 11, 2014

My father taught me how to play chess when I was five. When I was seven years old, I beat him for the first time. It felt wonderful, as you may imagine, a seven year old beating his own father, who was, well, ancient. And although I couldn't put it into words, my winning seemed like some kind of valuable Jungian lesson, or at the very least, a portent: youth triumphs over age, new replaces old in the grand march of civilization. Looking back on it now, however, now that he is gone and I am the ancient one, I have a slightly different take.

To begin with, I'm pretty sure I didn't actually win that game. In all probability he lost the game intentionally. I say this because I have a memory of bursting into tears whenever I lost, and also because, for my father, the game was never about winning so much as spending a contemplative afternoon with his son; he'd puff on his pipe and we'd listen to the Bach records he loved so much. To this day, whenever I catch a whiff of pipe tobacco or hear Johann Sebastian Bach on the radio or in an elevator, I get nostalgic. I also know from playing games with my own children and grandchildren that winning energizes them. They don't have to win all the time, but they like to win, and when they win, they naturally want to play more and thus become better.

There did come a pivotal point in my chess career when, even if he was doing his best, I started to beat him regularly. I don't know whether this is because I'd been practicing more, or I'd acquired some new skill through studying the games of the chess masters in the Encyclopedia Britannica, or whether he was in fact getting older and just couldn't concentrate the way he used to. Maybe all three. But what was fascinating was that as I won more often, the fact that I won meant less and less. Over time, what we did together morphed from a contest into a kind of dance. I would win, or he would win, it didn't matter.

My wife was raised with a completely different set of standards. Her father apparently never let the children win, and now as a result she doesn't like games of any kind. And she refuses to believe me when I say I don't care if I win or lose. So what this means is we don't play games together like many couples do. We talk and we read the newspaper over coffee. Oh, and we do crossword puzzles, that has become our passion. But crosswords, I've come to understand, are a strictly collaborative affair. They have much more in common with quilts and sweaters: they're about completion and fulfillment. Nobody wins, not the way we do them. And so, after grinding our brains into mush on a Sunday morning, when the moment arrives and we ink in the final answer, we just smile and give each other a gentle high five. A dance well done.

The Trouble With Harry
July 2009

The countdown has already begun for the seventh Harry Potter book, *Harry Potter and the Deathly Hallows*. Twenty-one days, no, twenty, no, well, it's going down and time is drawing nigh, and in the blink of a muggle's eye, copies of the Seventh and Final Harry Potter will be in everyone's homes and hands and beach bags everywhere.

This is, of course, a good thing. It will propel children further along down the yellow brick road of literature; it will be a boon to struggling bookstores; and it will give the whole world a breather from the horrors of Iraq and Darfur and whatever shenanigans Paris Hilton is up to.

Part of me wants Harry Potter to go on forever. I mean, why stop at seven? Why not seven more? Hey, I have titles all ready to go: Harry Potter and the Blue-Eyed Girl Next Door. Harry Potter and the Baby Who Never Learned to Sleep. Harry Potter and the Premature Bald Spot. Harry Potter Gets a Raise. (And the sequel) Harry Potter Gets Down-Sized. Harry Potter's 40th Hogwarts Reunion (where he recognizes no one). Harry Potter and the Lost Nursing Home in the Cotswolds.

Part of me would rejoice in this pageant of Potterdom. There is another part though, that says, with a heavy sigh, enough already. For Harry Potter to have any fictional juju left at all, the arc of his life and experience has to be checked and then brought to an appropriate close.

This is not to suggest that J. K. Rowling ought to have him whacked in the final episode, heaven forfend. Arthur Conan Doyle tried to do that to Sherlock Holmes, then, in response to his outraged fan base, brought him miraculously back to life. Big mistake. Harry does have to cease, however, because if he lives on, and Rowling stops writing about him as she has promised then, inevitably, the sharks will circle and other writers (some would call them hacks) will start to grind out further tawdry adventures. Harry's life would be diluted and, over time, his memory trashed. Could we really stand still for this? Reduce Harry to a pale comic strip? Lose him to the land of merchandising? Never.
Which is why, I'm afraid, that in the interest of literature and all that's true and

beautiful, we must confront reality. We must insist that *Harry Potter and the Deathly Hallows* be the last, we must hope that Harry rides off into some kind of mystical sunset, or that we turn a page and, like the *Sopranos*, everything goes suddenly black.

It's time. And our children deserve nothing less.

What Comes Next to Godliness, Do You Suppose?
April 14, 2012

It's spring now, the flowers are blooming, and whenever I look at the weather forecast, I think of a man named Tom and his quest for natural cleanliness. Many years ago, in an alternate universe, I worked in a clinic where I tried—with varying degrees of success—to help schizophrenics and other mentally ill people keep their lives in order. The other day, in the midst of one of Northern California's more intense downpours, I got to thinking about one of my former clients. I'll call him Tom, because his name was something like that, and also because I'm the Emperor of the Bookstore, and naming people in essays is one of the few perks we Emperors enjoy. Tom was an affable fellow—very polite, very well-spoken. Sometimes he could be a little disheveled-looking, and, if you listened to him go on for a while, a bit full of himself. But at first glance you probably wouldn't suspect that he had a mental health problem. What tipped you off, however, was this: Tom had trouble bathing. Specifically, he would only bathe in rain water or, once in a blue moon, in a river. Never a shower, never a tub. It was something to do with purity, he said. This was not an issue in Massachusetts during the spring and summer months, when it rained often and rivers weren't frozen and thus readily available. But after October, it was a trial to be alone in a room with him.

I bring this up not to disparage poor Tom, but as a way of thinking about all of our habits and how close we all are on a continuum of being crazy. Basically, someone is deemed crazy in this culture when his or her actions appear to put someone at risk. Tom refused to bathe, which meant that he could not get hired or hold down a job or interact successfully with his fellow human beings. Without income and human contact he was, ipso facto, at risk, and, therefore, crazy.

In America, where everyone is a stranger to everyone else, we are forever shifting the tea leaves to determine who is friend and who is foe, who is sane and who is mad. Some of us are better at this kind of discernment than others, but when you add a gun to the mix it leads almost inevitably to tragedies, such as what happened to Trayvon Martin in Florida.

I don't profess to know what happened that night in Sanford, Florida, except that a child who was walking home with a bag of Skittles in his hand is dead.

There may have been reasons, circumstances, all that. But Martin was not armed, and Zimmerman, who was following him, had a gun. And someone stepped over the line into crazy.

Orwell was an Optimist
May 2003

There has been a good bit of noise last month in the paper and down at City Hall about the Patriot Act, whether we should support it, or oppose it, or even if we have any business discussing it at all. City officials, according to some pundits, should not comment on a federal government policy which may or may not be constitutional. Unless, of course, you happen to be a constitutional scholar, in which case you probably already have a regular gig on CNN, so what are you doing loitering around Sonoma in the first place?

However, since neither Lilla nor I work for the government (or against it, for that matter), and since the Patriot Act actually has the potential to impact our business and your freedom to read whatever you like, I feel entitled to open my mouth.

Bookstores and libraries are on the front lines when it comes to this legislation. How so? Well, suppose you bought a book from us on, say, how to build a nuclear bomb (I doubt that something like that exists, but just humor me). And then say the FBI came around and wanted to know what you bought. Not only would we have to tell them, but we could not tell you or anyone else (except a lawyer) that they were even in the store. Well, you say, a maniac who wants a book on building nuclear bombs deserves what he or she gets, right? But what if it wasn't so obviously a threat to planetary peace? What if you had cancer and wanted a book on growing marijuana to ease the pain of chemotherapy? Or suppose you needed a guide to getting a sex change operation? Or a book on how to tell your parents that you are gay? Or what if you take a sudden interest in learning Arabic or converting to Islam? The FBI could ask us about anything you buy. I repeat: anything. It is an unlimited license to spy. And a government that spies on its own people sends an Orwellian chill over the land. The message is clear: you're not as free today as you were yesterday.

Granted, these are tough times we are going through, and perhaps tough times call for tough measures. But I think back on other times—Pearl Harbor, for example, and the incarceration of the Japanese: how we apologized later for the pain we visited upon an innocent group of immigrants and their descendants. I also remember the early days of the Cold War, when many other innocent folks were caught up in a web of groundless suspicion, their lives ruined because of clubs they'd joined or lectures they'd attended years earlier. The ironic (some would say tragic) thing is that we've been through all this before and we still never seem to learn from our mistakes. I know people are scared. I know the terror index color code is yellow or orange or whatever. And, in my heart of hearts, I feel as patriotic as the next guy, but at the end of the day, I'd like to be sure that the constitution I'm defending is still worth the paper it is printed on.

How Lucky We Are
September 29, 2012

If you happen to pass by Readers' Books this week, you'll notice a crowded montage of black and white photos in the window. Stop and inspect them, and you'll realize that they are all famous authors from different times and places. And then you will no doubt read the sign beneath them that says "These writers and others were silenced by people who were afraid." Ironically, some writers came into their own as a result of being banned. That's how they are often remembered: it's not the books so much but the controversy their books engendered that lingers on in the public's imagination. Think Charles Bukowski and Henry Miller and Alan Ginsberg, and how well they succeeded in upsetting their puritanical universe.

Ginsberg and Miller may have been in the forefront, but the truth is that many more writers have had their books censored and removed from libraries than you may know. And these were often not firebrands but thoughtful, gentle souls who just happen to have had something to say which was at odds with a given community. J.K. Rowling, for example, the lady who wrote the Harry Potter series, has been frequently assailed by Christian fundamentalists because they have it in their heads that the magical power of Harry and his fellow wizards is akin to satanism. And our own local guy, Jack London, had his work roundly attacked because people thought he was a socialist. He was, but so what?

This is the 30th anniversary of Banned Books Week, and so we celebrate those brave people who wrote and struggled mightily to get their point of view out in the open. And if you care at all about the ongoing issue of free speech, I urge you to also take a look at the new book by Salman Rushdie, his memoir entitled *Joseph Anton*. Rushdie's novel *The Satanic Verses*, you will recall, earned him a death sentence from the Ayatollah Khomeini in Iran and forced him to go into hiding. *Joseph Anton* is the true story of how he managed to live under those nerve-wracking circumstances and how, after nine years, he has emerged with a profound understanding of what it really means to live by your words. We can all learn something valuable from this.

To the Ramparts with Captain Underpants
September 2013

It's September again, which signals a lot of things to a lot of people. Back to school, and the Jewish New Year festivities (although, let's be honest, we don't really get all that festive..."fastive" is more like it). For booksellers, September traditionally means we're sailing into Banned Books Week, a time to reflect on America's time-honored propensity for shooting the messenger.

Turns out, there's a whole New York Public Library's worth of books that some folks have found objectionable at one time or another. After almost a quarter of a century, you'd think I'd know most of the offending titles by heart, but when I checked recently, I found a bunch of books that struck me as just plain bizarre. Beyond the usual suspects—Henry Miller, William Burroughs, James Joyce—beyond the Harry Potter books, which some fundamentalists deem satanic, beyond *Fifty Shades of Grey*, which, in this age of internet porn is about as racy as Sesame Street, there are a host of unredeemable books you've probably never imagined.

Consider, for example, the ever popular Captain Underpants. This is a series of cartoon books for youngsters, aged 4-8, wherein irreverent subjects like going to the potty, nose picking, nudity, pie throwing, giving people wedgies, and other silliness is discussed at length. Anyone who has ever raised a child through those years knows good and well that that's what interests them, that's what makes them laugh, and that's what they love to read about. In fact, the only adults who might complain about such things are those who've never had children, or perhaps are so stuck in the mud they won't ever admit to picking their nose.

There are other books, too, that surprise and dismay. Would you believe that *The Glass Castle* is on the list? *The Glass Castle*, by Jeannette Walls, is a wonderful memoir about someone going through an absolutely horrific childhood and yet somehow emerging triumphant. Her parents are well-meaning but lost in their dreams, so lost they often lose sight of their children and how to care for them. But more than their errors, it's a book about resilience, which is a quality all of us should be storing up in vast quantities. I can't figure out who would object to this story; I mean, if you hated this book, you probably would be down on the life of Lincoln, too. He wasn't exactly raised at the Ritz, either.

The list of banned books is extensive, but the good news is that while these books are sometimes pulled from shelves, they ultimately find their way into the public sphere. Many of them are best sellers, and many are required reading for high school and college. Just as the Chinese couldn't stop the nomadic invaders by building a wall, neither can prudes and other self-righteous types stop the spread of books and ideas. That's why Banned Books Week is worth remembering. That's why we do what we do.

We're All Doing What We Can
January 28, 2012

Sometime during the last great recession, I found myself in a discussion with a fellow bookseller. This took place at one of our conventions in Oakland or Chicago, I can't remember where exactly, but this guy was complaining to me about people shoplifting books from his store. "I have to watch them [his customers] like a hawk," he said. To which I replied: "I think I would be flattered if someone actually stole something. At least they'd have the joy of reading. And who knows where that can lead."

He didn't appreciate my feeble attempt at humor, but part of me wasn't kidding. If someone needs a book so badly that he/she has no other recourse but to steal it, I would be all right with that. Which brings me to a wonderful piece I read this morning by Nicholas Kristof. It was all about a poor, tough, black kid in the Arkansas school system of the 1950's named Olly Neal, a kid who talked back to his teachers and was clearly destined to go to prison someday. This Olly Neal found himself in the school library one day and saw a book by Frank Yerby with a very risque cover on it . He wanted to check it out, but then he thought, if I do, then the other kids will know that I'm reading and my reputation will suffer. So instead of checking out, he did what any self-respecting teenage thug would do: he stole it. He took it home and read it cover to cover and found that it delighted him. A few days later, he returned with the idea of slipping the book back on the shelf. And there, in the same place, he found another Frank Yerby title. So he stole that, too. The next week he came back with the purloined book, and lo and behold, another Frank Yerby. All together Olly stole, read, and returned four Frank Yerby books, and through them came a sudden and irrepressible love of reading. Olly went on to graduate, go to college, and become a lawyer. His kids picked up his love of reading and have made successful lives for themselves. What Olly didn't know until later was that the librarian, Mildred Grady, had spotted him stealing that first Frank Yerby. She was going to confront him, but then she thought, no, if he wants that book so badly, then let him have it. Not only that, but Ms. Grady (who was also poor and black and working in a dead-end segregated school system) took the trouble to drive 70 miles to Memphis and purchased another Frank Yerby book with her own money, which she put on the shelf for him. She was the one secretly supplying the books to Olly Neal and her selfless gesture is what probably saved his life.

I offer this story not as a way to puff myself up, but to suggest that none of us ever really know what the effect of our random acts of kindness may be. I know my responsibility, however, and what gives me the greatest joy.

There'll Always be an England
January 2010

Each year our colleagues at the New Oxford American Dictionary select what they call the "word of the year"—some piece of jargon that has significantly altered the English language. This year they chose the word "unfriend," which means to remove someone as a "friend" on a social networking site such as Facebook.

The competition for this honor was fierce, apparently; the judges had to wade through terms like "funemployed" (people taking advantage of their new unemployed status to have fun), "delebs" (dead celebrities), and "tramp stamp" (a tattoo on the lower back, usually on a woman).

I have to admit that I find this whole exercise both bewildering and annoying. Of course any language worth its salt is always growing and changing, and perhaps we should take note of this from time to time. But that is different than holding a full-blown awards ceremony.

And this year's word, in my humble opinion, makes a mockery of something that lies at the heart of Anglo-Saxon sensibilities. Friend, which probably stems from an Old English amalgam of freon (to love) and freo (free) is, by any estimate, a big word. You needed friends in the brutish world of ancient Britain. Friends were like air or water. Without friends to help you hunt and build a fire and beat off your foes you could (would, more than likely) die.

To "unfriend" therefore would seem to carry weight, even in the abstract world of the internet. But alas, it does not. These days people "friend" and "unfriend" one another as casually as we change lanes on the freeway. And what exactly does it mean to "unfriend" a person? Is that person thenceforth an enemy? Less than human? If you drop somebody off your social radar, is your world improved? Purified? There are no clear answers to any of this. What is clear is that "friend" does not mean "friend" in the traditional sense anymore, and true friends might well be offended if they were suddenly looped into the same company as the kid who delivers your newspaper or someone who sat behind you, fifty years ago, in the second grade.

I have a few people who I think of as friends. They are, for the most part, folks I have known a long time. We share a narrative and a lifetime's worth of values. And I worry about watering down these relationships by adding in a bunch of folks I met once at the beach.

In the end, language matters. Definitions matter. Content matters. That's why I think it's always better to read a ten page short story by Borges as opposed to three hundred pages of Danielle Steel. Life is short, after all—as the Druids used to say.

Progress
July 2006

Even the most casual observer has to be troubled by what's going on in the Bay Area book business these days. A few months back, Kepler's Books of Palo Alto abruptly closed its doors, then, with the prodding and clamor and good will of the local populace, reopened them. Then we read about how Barnes & Noble is moving its megastore in Corte Madera to a spot which just happens to be a stone's throw from Book Passage, one of the flagship independent bookstores of California. Next, word came that A Clean, Well-Lighted Place for Books in San Francisco is folding, and most recently, there is the sad news that Cody's Books on Telegraph Avenue in Berkeley is closing its doors on July 10th.

There are reasons for these happenings, of course. Traffic patterns shift. Partnerships dissolve. Like everyone else, booksellers eventually get tired, burnt-out. Until now, however, the Bay Area has managed to remain more or less immune to the clear-cutting that has been the fate of independent booksellers around the country.

As for Cody's, they have a satellite operation on Fourth Street—a trendier area, and also a large new store they have just launched in San Francisco, which is, by any estimate, a big bet. They are, in other words, stretched. And, as anyone who has walked down Telegraph Avenue in the last ten years can tell you, it ain't what it used to be. Parking is a headache and the local street people do not, alas, add to the ambiance. But to me, the demise of Cody's on Telegraph feels bad. Cody's was where students and poets and philosophers used to hang out. It was a romantic experience to visit Cody's and check out the new books. Cody's had virtually everything; whatever was hip was out on the shelves at Cody's before anywhere else, it seemed. And now they're going to close. What can I say? It feels bad, it hurts.

The buying habits of Americans used to be fixed around a civil (and civilizing) human experience: you shopped where you knew the clerks and they knew you. People took care of one another. There would be the usual exchange of pleasantries—you'd find out if the owner's daughter made the swim team and he in turn would wonder whatever became of your Aunt Agnes whose house caught fire. He'd gift wrap a present for your dad and offer to take it to the post office, while you'd tell him the new joke you heard in line at the bank that morning. That's the way it used to be. Now, an ever increasing segment of this country does not read at all, or, if they do, they shop online for books, getting what they want anonymously. They don't have to say hello to anyone. They don't have to smile. They just click and go. What a relief.

I suppose my larger point is that with each individual bookstore that closes, we are chipping steadily away at the world, which, until now, has sustained and nourished us. And not just bookstores. A few years ago, we happened to be in Beloit, Wisconsin, where my son went to college. Beloit had been a paper mill town. It may still be, although there is precious little evidence of that. In fact, just about the only thriving business around was a giant Walmart a few miles away. The old downtown was a sad procession of empty storefronts for lease. This is what some folks call progress. I call it a blight. And a shame.

What's Your Name? Take a Number.
September 2005

For as long as I can remember, I've had an uncomfortable relationship with machines. I never owned a transistor radio, even though it was once the rage. I was not, like my two sons, eager to drive a car, even though it meant freedom from my parents and easier access to girls. I did not take naturally to the computer when it first arrived, and only recently caved in to the necessity of a cell phone. You could say I don't want to be connected, and I can still remember a time when people who walked around talking to themselves were looked at askance. Nowadays, of course, psychotics can pass as ordinary Joes just by pretending to be talking on a cell phone, so maybe that's one of those unintended consequences of technology for which we can rejoice, I don't know.

What I do know is that machinery and bureaucrats (people who are forced to act like machines) are forever getting in the way of normal human enterprise.

A few years ago, for instance, I was on my way to work and decided to sample the new Taco Bell in town. Now, mind you, I almost never eat in such places; but it was brand new and I thought, well, I'll try it just to be neighborly...so I walked in. It was early and the place was deserted. There was a Mexican woman in the kitchen area (clearly the cook) and there was a teenage girl in a Taco Bell uniform standing behind the counter, which was in front of one of those long rope-like mazes you see at airports and banks. Obviously they were expecting huge throngs for tacos, but at this hour there was, alas, no one. I went through the maze, glanced at the menu board and ordered a breakfast burrito. The girl nodded solemnly, wrote something down and passed it over to the Mexican woman. When I paid her, she gave me a receipt and announced that my number was 638. The Mexican woman did her stuff, put the meal in a styrofoam tray, passed it forward to the teenager, who then walked back to the counter and in a loud, booming voice, called "638!" I looked around. Still no one in the restaurant. "That must be me," I said.

Airports abound in this kind of inanity. I remember reading about Bill Bryson, the well-known travel writer, who, after living in England for years, returned to his native America and tried to board a plane without a driver's license. Naturally, our ever-alert security people stopped him. Who are you? They asked. "Well,

I'm an author, my name is Bryson." And then he pulled out the copy of his latest book and showed him his picture on the inside jacket. "See? That's me." But they still wouldn't let him board because an author's photo on a book was not one of the approved forms of identification. "Well," he said (and I'm paraphrasing here), "do you honestly think I would go to all the time and trouble and heartache of writing a book and getting it printed just so I could walk in here and fool you guys into thinking I'm not who I am? Is that what you think?"

The point is, of course, that they don't think. They are not paid to think, merely to follow the rules.

Small independent bookstore folks, on the other hand, think just to stay alive. They are, if they are worth their salt, human beings who care about the wants and needs of other human beings. They may use machines from time to time, but they aren't run by machines. The passing on of a book into the hands of a customer is often a sacred act; money is almost an afterthought, which is probably why so few booksellers ever become millionaires.

I am, by the way, not averse to becoming a millionaire. I imagine I would be able to handle it, that it wouldn't alter my personality too severely. A new car would be nice. A better house, okay. Maybe a trip to someplace exotic now and then. My real needs are few. I don't even want to retire, although I think about it occasionally. Retire? Retire to what? What would I do? Hey, I know, maybe go work behind the counter at Taco Bell. Now there's an idea…

Don't Even Think About Going Home Again
October 6, 2012

Some people remember their high school years fondly. For them it was a simple, innocent, rose-colored time when kids held hands as they ambled down the hallways, a time of girlish crushes and tongue-tied boys with pimples. That image changed when, recently, I happened upon a brochure from the local junior college detailing their fall curriculum. In it was a class titled: "The Sixties: A History." Now wait just a minute, I thought snarkily. That's not history, I lived through that. I remember the Beatles and bell bottoms and tie-dyed tee shirts and the whole mad world coming apart over Vietnam and Civil Rights. How can they even think of summarizing that? It's only been, what, fifty years, right? Half a century?

And I was on the cusp of reclaiming my wild, wonderful youth, but then just the other day someone talked me into going online and discovering what my classmates from 1965 were up to, and that's when everything became crystal clear. First, you must understand: my high school class had over 1300 people, so I only knew a handful of them. Others were just names that kind of, sort of, rang a bell. Oh yeah, him. And then, through the magic of the internet, these names from the past began appearing in my email, wanting to contact me and leaving me cryptic messages. Someone named Tom wrote, "Hey Andy, you're great. I was never that mean, was I?" Uh, no, I don't think so, I said to myself. Whoever you are.

Memory, like almost everything else in America, has become an enormous business. Even as we speak, corporations are busy marketing your picture in the yearbook to other lost and lonely souls with whom you shared an algebra class long ago. Maybe this is harmless fun. I can imagine, after all, that there are some for whom high school was the absolute pinnacle of their life. Maybe they want to relive something. I am not one of them, I realize now. And the truth is, even if I could remember who these people were, in my heart of hearts, I probably don't care what they're doing now that they're eligible for Medicare and Social Security. After fifty years, things change. At least you hope so.

Where Is the Plug to the Hole in My Heart
August 18, 2012

I'm over it now, but for the better part of last week, I found myself crawling around in the dust under my desk, trying to disconnect and reconnect cables and routers and modems and back-up batteries. You should know that underneath my desk it's dark. You might also be amused to learn that there are all manner of disgusting things that have settled there and found a home over time—post-it notes and paper clips and rubber bands and bits and pieces of Thai take-out, not to mention all the miscellaneous wires.

And the reason I bring this stuff up is, ironically, because I don't want to talk about it. I didn't go into the book trade in order to become a computer tech genius, no, far from it. I don't even much care for computers, truth be told. When they're working, it's fine, but when they stop it suddenly becomes your (my) responsibility to know everything there is to know about them. Full disclosure: I have the exact same issue with washing machines, televisions, and cars. I just want the damn things to work, and shoot me, kill me—I don't care what goes on under the hood. Is this a morally reprehensible opinion? I don't think so.

I suspect many of you are in the same position: with every new day, the brave new world we've all bought into requires a whole generation of wizards (usually 15 year-olds) to repair and maintain it, and all we can do is throw up our hands in despair.

I don't mind writing a check to someone who knows more than I do. I've come to the conclusion that there are lots of things I don't know, and that's okay. What troubles me more, though, is that, in the words of my neighbor, we have all become janitors. We aren't doing at all what we thought we would do in life; we're just cleaning up after our broken machines and the Byzantine infrastructure that was supposed to make things so simple. Bankers spend their days wading through and wriggling out of regulations. Pharmacists are on the phone to Manila and India trying to get total strangers working for insurance companies to okay a prescription for someone in California. I thought I was put on earth to sell books, not crawl around for hours under my desk looking for a plug that doesn't exist.

I was wrong. There now. I admit it.

The Jolt of Human Kindness
January 11, 2014

We are big believers in birthdays here at Readers' Books. (I suppose you don't have to be a big believer since they happen regardless, but still, we believe.) Each time one rolls around, our staff gets together and ponies up money for a joint present for the lucky (inevitable) recipient, we wrap it in our finest gift wrap (translation: whatever's available at the moment), we steal one of our notecards, and take turns signing and writing silly things about how much we appreciate the birthday person. Then, on the approximate day of birth, we secretly mass together and, when they least expect it, we burst into song in front of him or her. I say "approximate" because often the object of our singing is off that day, so we have to fudge that a bit.

The birthday song is de rigeur, but it turns out, not everyone sings the birthday song. In particular, Thea is consistently adamant about not singing. Chalk it off to terminal shyness or lack of musical praise growing up. The theories abound, but most of the time she will stand there and smile while the rest of us make fools of ourselves. A few years ago I made her recite "Happy birthday to you, happy birthday to you, happy birthday dear (I forget who), happy birthday to you." This caused gales of laughter, naturally, and while she still won't sing, I feel, as her resident therapist, that with this new approach we've made significant progress.

The birthday song lyrics are, to be sure, inane, but it's the heartfelt thought that counts, and no one here has more good heartfelt thoughts than Thea.

Our birthday celebrations last maybe two minutes at most, but that doesn't mean they aren't intense and wonderful. We laugh and sing and express our love for one another. Then boom—it's back to work. Think of it as one of those 5-hour energy drinks. A sudden jolt of human kindness. That's what we're all about. If you are ever lucky enough to see one of our birthdays (and not many customers do) let me just say, you can die happy. But not before your next birthday, I hope.

Some People Only Talk about the Weather.
March 17, 2012

I have a little blue notebook that I refer to frequently. It contains mundane information such as how much money we took in on a given day and what author was speaking that evening. I've also taken to adding what you might call extraneous information, such as if it was the day of the Superbowl or Easter Sunday, or if on that morning a couple of planes happened to crash into the World Trade Center. All these matters are beyond my control and who knows, could affect business. The other thing I have been dutifully watching is the weather. If it's cold, for example, I mark that with a C. Hot is an H and if it's raining, of course, R. There aren't too many C days in Sonoma, thankfully, and H only hits around August and September. R, on the other hand, can be a big deal.

The thing about R, I've found, is not the R itself, but the way it Rs. If you wake up in the morning and it looks like it's going to R, that probably won't stop you from getting dressed and going downtown to do your errands. Even if it starts R-ing en route, that's okay. If, however, you wake up and it's pouring cats and dogs, chances are you'll burrow down under the covers. Maybe you'll figure out that those errands downtown weren't so pressing after all. You didn't really need to go to the bookstore. Heck, you've still got another 500 pages of *Don Quixote* sitting right there on your bedside table (never mind that you've already determined that *Don Quixote* is boring and unreadable, it's there, it's free, and best of all, it's dry). Another factoid I've learned about R days: If it Rs relentlessly for a couple of days, things slow down at the bookstore. But if it continues to R day after day, sooner or later everyone shrugs, pulls their umbrellas out of the closet and tries to get on with their lives. They make peace with the R, in other words; they don't forget about the R; and now, thanks to their pluck and unmeltable spirit, it is no longer an impediment.

This is the kind of science we booksellers and all other retailers secretly engage in. We have amassed years of data on this subject and we like to think we know what we're talking about. Where we come from, R is no laughing matter, you see. Nor H, nor C.

You May Not be Familiar with this Mystical World
April 23, 2012

Every year about this time, a pang of nostalgia sweeps over me and I start to wax poetic about my good friends, the people who work here. Those deeply loyal and apparently tireless souls, each so brilliant in his or her own right, many of whom have been shuffling around this place year in and year out for little money. What motivates them? I wake up wondering at 3:00 a.m. What siren song do they hear at dawn that jolts them out of bed and shoves them—even without their morning coffee—through the bookstore door? And then I ask myself the next question, which I dare not pose to them: Are you crazy?

It used to be that many rational people entered the book business. It had its ups and downs, of course, and an occasional dark side as well, but, in the main, you could call yourself a bookseller and earn a living and not have to fret that the chattering class would raise their collective eyebrows in dismay. That was before Barnes & Noble and Borders and Amazon and ebooks. Before publishers started treating books as products, dumb things, of no more importance than deodorant or chewing gum. Before the deluge, in other words. It was a simpler, more reverent world then, and, now, looking back on it, perhaps a better one.

In the last twenty years the world of books has changed beyond recognition, and still, there is this unending stream of people seeking employment, eager to put their alphabetical skills to work sorting and shelving, all pumped up to expound on what they stayed up late to read and couldn't get enough of, happy just to dust and file and, God willing, to sell a few books here and there.

It looks like madness, but it's not. What I've come to realize is that while they would all dearly love to take home decent paychecks and have a health insurance plan that offers more than a Bandaid and a shoulder to cry on, the folks who successfully take root in bookstores like ours are, first and foremost, dreamers. They have inner lives that are as rich and convoluted as any labyrinth, and being in a bookstore offers them the time and space and, most importantly, the nourishment they need for their spiritual journey. That's why they're really here: to work on the mystical narrative of their lives. And in their own special way, to heal the planet, one story at a time.

Where Do We Go From Here
August 11, 2012

Last Sunday, while scientists and engineers at the Jet Propulsion Lab in Pasadena were cheering and celebrating how they'd managed to land a craft on the surface of Mars, in a Sikh temple near Milwaukee, a deranged Neo-Nazi shot six worshippers to death before he killed himself. The first event was joyful and triumphant, while the second clearly called for outrage and despair. And the fact that they both occurred almost simultaneously got me thinking about the distance we humans have travelled since we first walked out of Africa.

Science seems to know no bounds; the men and women who do the math and peer into microscopes and experiment with complex equations have only one real goal in mind—to further our knowledge, which, it is hoped, will ultimately redound to mankind's benefit. Oh, there may be one or two "evil" scientists out there, the kind conjured up in James Bond movies, but the overwhelming aim of science has always been the advancement of civilized behavior.

The same cannot be said of what happened in Wisconsin. We don't know for certain why this lone individual suddenly opened fire on the Sikhs, though circumstantial evidence points to racism, the impulse to protect and defend your clan against another. Racism isn't something that's carefully reasoned out. It's like a primitive gene we've never quite been able to locate. It's all about the "other" in our midst. Ultimately, it's about trying to kill the mystery, the bogeyman, whoever or whatever it is we don't know. In that sense it is the antithesis of science. It needn't matter that Sikhs or Muslims or blacks or Jews or Mexicans are no immediate threat; to a racist, their mere existence in the universe constitutes a threat.

As a member of a minority I take these kinds of incidents personally. Thousands of years of history have taught me that fine words and lofty intentions—even good gun laws—do not guarantee safety. We say we mean well, but sometimes it's not enough. In addition to freedom and democracy America has, from its inception, generated a clear and unrelenting drumbeat of violence toward the "other." Open Howard Zinn's *People's History of the United States* to almost any page and you'll see what a nightmarish rollercoaster it's been. Now, you could argue that the fact that someone named Barack Obama is our President today suggests we've come a long way in the direction of tolerance, and I wouldn't disagree. But neither would I rest on my laurels. I'd very much like to think that the arc of history is moving more towards Mars than Wisconsin, but only time—and our concerted efforts—will tell.

Guns and Butts: A Modest Comparison
July 28, 2012

In ancient times, when I worked in a pharmacy in Pasadena, it was standard practice to sell, right up front by the candy counter, and right along side the vitamins and cod liver oil bottles and sanitary pads, I know you kids will never believe this, but—cigarettes! That's right, cigarettes, those things which, if you use them as instructed, will, over time, kill you. Now granted, back then in the 50's and 60's there were some doctors who (for a modest fee) would say that cigarettes didn't kill you; rather it was you who killed yourself by using your own free will to smoke those darn cigarettes. And, of course, the tobacco lobby owned half the United States Congress, so passing any laws or taxes or regulations that might tamp down demand, well, that ran right in the face of free enterprise and no patriotic American would tolerate that, no sirree bob.

I remember getting into a long argument with the manager of the pharmacy around this issue, when I said in my snarky, teenage way, "Don't you think it's just a little bit incongruous for a pharmacy—which is supposedly all about health—to be promoting cigarettes?"

The problem of cigarettes sounds just like another problem we're currently up against: gun violence. Now I know that the 2nd Amendment gives us the right to own a gun. That's fine. But let's get real, folks: there are a lot of confused and frightened people out there. There are some crazy people who know beyond a shadow of a doubt that our President is a communist or a Muslim or from outer space. There are grown men who go off in the woods and play army. And there are also something like 300 million guns floating around loose. This may be perfectly legal, but, by any other standard, it's bad chemistry. In 2010, the last year for which we have solid statistical information, there were some 12,000 murders in the United States, of which 8,775 were carried out courtesy of guns. This is roughly the entire population of Sonoma decimated in a single year. It's more folks than we lost in Iraq and Afghanistan. And it goes on, year after year. And people just shrug. Nothing to be done. Guns don't kill people, says the president of the NRA. People kill people. But, oddly enough, in places where there are fewer guns, fewer people get killed.

It took time, but we were somehow able to make a big dent in the cigarette problem. No one is afraid of the tobacco lobby anymore. People go outside now when they absolutely have to smoke. The world is a better place in that sense. I don't see why the same thing can't happen with guns.

Willy Loman is Not Your Friend
November 24, 2012

For the last 30 years or so of her life, my mother had a robust and extensive relationship with the television in her living room. Well, not with the television, exactly, but with the people who lived inside the television. They were her friends: Archie Bunker, Bea Arthur, Mary Tyler Moore, Dick Van Dyke, all the folks on *Seinfeld*. Their lives, their foibles and adventures, played a significant part in how she viewed her own life. This is probably not a rarity; no doubt many people of all ages get drawn into make-believe worlds that are funnier, happier, less stressful than their own. That's fiction, after all, and it's a useful part of life.

But it got me to thinking about how much of my world is devoted to people who don't really exist. I still have certain nostalgic ties to existential characters like Mrs. Bridge in Evan McConnell's novel of the same name, or Willy Loman from *Death of a Salesman*, or Gogo and Didi in *Waiting for Godot*. I still feel the angst of some of Philip Roth's tortured Jewish souls. I still gravitate towards the cool phrasing and suave mannerisms of people like Raymond Chandler and John le Carré. But none of the characters in those books are my friends. They might be mentors in some subtle way, they may instruct me about situations, but I would never think of them with affection. Maybe that's the difference between friends in print and friends on the screen. Maybe you just know too much about the people you read about to love them without reservation.

My mother's "friends" were nice enough, I suppose. I remember laughing at their antics when I sat with her watching. But I also remember wanting more from them, some unexpected tic or lingering thought or misstep that would turn them into more than characters in a script. Literature, it seems to me, should be about more than just clever devices for moving a plot from A to B. Literature should have some enduring impact; literature should lead you out of the abyss. And in that sense, characters in literature cannot be your friends; you wouldn't want them to be your friends. No, they are far more important than that.

The Big Switcheroo
March 2003

The vote is in on our Big Switcheroo from one side of the street to another, and I am happy to report that most folks—most, but not all—are at peace with what we've done.

I want to say a word to those three or four individuals who did not approve, and who were courageous or indignant enough to say something. Yes, it looks different. Yes, it may not be quite as charming as the three little rooms we had before. For many people change is difficult to embrace.

My own mother hates change. When her family moved from Savannah to New York City in the middle of the Depression, she pined for years for her lost home in Dixie. When she and my dad moved to Pasadena in 1954, she decided she hated it and, at the same moment, started missing New York with the same stubborn, rear-view mirror passion she'd felt for Savannah. And when they moved to the Bay Area years later, it was Pasadena she suddenly missed. Go figure.

I can't argue about aesthetics or nostalgia. But after eleven years of trying to run a bookstore out of three cramped rooms there are surely more efficient ways of doing things. In the old store, for example, special orders were behind the counter, but because of the way the windows were positioned the books were on shelves at floor level. This meant that they'd get dinged by errant feet or sprinkled on by occasional coffee cups. It also meant that whoever went looking for them had to get down on his or her hands and knees. Let me tell you something: my knees are not the pliable creatures they once were.

And allow me to share with you a tiny anecdote that speaks volumes. A woman came up to the counter just the other day with an armload of kid's books. "I didn't know you sold children's books," she said. "How long have you been shopping here?" I asked. "Seven years," she said. Right then, a lightbulb went off in my head. In seven years, I realized, she'd never once visited those other rooms we had across the street. And I'll bet she's not alone in her habits.

The new space is much more efficient. You can see everything we have to offer.

It's bustling. It's economical. I think it's charming already, but in time it will be even more so.

When people ask me why we did this, the answer is simple. The truth is that last year, Readers' Books caught a heavy dose of the recession that the rest of America has been suffering from, and rather than sit around and hope that things will improve we decided to act.

I'm thankful that most people appreciate the need to make alterations. For those few holdouts who still have trouble with it, I can only hope you've never met my mother. Whatever she has might be contagious.

Ticktock Talk
September 2012

I've been trying to live in real time lately, which hasn't been easy. This is because the truth is, most of my day is spent juggling the future. There are great moral questions out there without answers, dark dilemmas wrapped in even darker enigmas which I often just have to guess at. For example, which bills must I pay promptly? Which ones can I put off for a week or two or ten? Which ones can I shave down to a fraction of their size and still not be put on credit hold? And are there any bills out there that I may ultimately ignore? (No, there are not.)

Somehow, I have been elevated into this managerial world, and while I'm getting pretty good at it, I can't yet say it's a natural fit. After all, in my previous incarnation at Readers' Books, my jobs were simple: I sold the books, I returned the books, and most important of all, I told the jokes. Now I have to do all that plus fifteen other things, like paying the bills.

People often say they want to work here because they just love to read, but this passion, while admirable, is largely misplaced. Bookselling is not about reading; bookselling is about schlepping boxes of books from here to there, and, by hook or by crook, paying for those self-same books. In between schlepping books and paying for them, there are those brief, glorious, theatrical moments when books are actually discussed and lovingly sold. This is not to demean the process: Of course you need to unpack them and display them and then pack them up again to go back to the publishers when nobody wants them anymore. And of course you must pay for them and hopefully have a little left over for the groceries. This is not a bad thing, it's just ma-and-pa capitalism. Still, if I had my druthers, and if I had any time at all (real or otherwise), I'd rather be telling jokes.

A Word to the Wise
July 27, 2013

Many years ago, when I was a young man, I had a great gig teaching English in Japan. Even though they are an island nation and far, far away from the English-speaking world, the Japanese like to latch on to Western habits; young girls would sometimes on a Sunday afternoon put on crinolines and dance in the park to the sounds of Buddy Holly, while their male counterparts varoomed around on motorcycles in the manner of James Dean. Others (older men in berets, generally) would spend evenings in overpriced coffee houses listening to Miles Davis records. They think of themselves as cosmopolitan, in other words, and learning to converse in English is one of those hip obsessions many folks there have. There are English clubs and private classes in conversational English, and, of course, virtually every child is put into an after-school English school (they call them juku) where they spend hour after hour reciting all manner of trivial sentences: What is your favorite fruit? My favorite fruit is apple. My favorite fruit is cherry. My favorite fruit is lemon. (One kid actually said that.)

We don't seem to do a lot of that around here. Maybe we don't feel the need because, after all, pretty much everyone speaks English, don't they? And English is already the corporate language of the planet, so let's just sit back and wait for the mountain to come to Mohammed, so to speak. Well, as someone who loves languages, loves the lilt and flow and subtle meanings of words, I have to say that I find this notion disturbing.

English is a fine language, mind you, but there are so many other beautiful tongues, with so much poetry and wisdom to impart to us, we're surely doing ourselves a disservice by our self-centered disinterest. And as a practical matter, it's just plain stupid. Given the way our demographics are changing in California, it's only a matter of years (maybe months) before street signs in Spanish and Chinese are on an equal footing with English ones.

I guess what I'm saying is, it's way past high time we joined the rest of the civilized world and started learning their languages—not because we're inevitably doomed to be overrun by Chinese business moguls, not because the Latino population is destined to outproduce us "baby-wise," but just because there are only so many resources here to go around, and the spaces between us on this globe are growing smaller and smaller; like it or not, we're all part of the same crumbling neighborhood now, and neighbors need to understand one another.

Which brings to mind an old Yiddish proverb: "Sleep faster, we need the pillows." This sounds a lot better in the original, of course. But how would you know?

Life Savers
July 2004

A few years back, Lilla and I attended one of those bookselling conferences where people regularly sit around and bemoan the fate of books and publishers and, of course, their own miserable brick-and-mortar worlds. At this particular get-together, we were treated to a breakfast talk by Victor Villasenor, author of *Rain and Gold*. Mr. Villasenor grew up on the streets of San Diego, a poor Chicano with no future beyond jail or an early violent death. As a teenager, he was starting to get into trouble with the cops, he admitted, and his life would have ended badly had it not been for an encounter with, of all people, a bookseller. He was wandering through a bookstore and, on a whim, asked the owner for a recommendation. What do you like to read? asked the bookseller. I don't know, he replied, because, although he knew how, to tell the truth, he couldn't remember a single book he'd ever read. In the end, the bookseller gave him a Hemingway title to try. Young Villasenor took it home and read it, then returned the following week for another suggestion. This went on for several years and, slowly, over time, an amazing transformation occurred. He found meaning in his own life and began to write himself. When his first book, *Macho!* was published, he received five complimentary copies from the publisher. The first thing he did was go straight over to the bookstore. He walked up to his old friend, the owner, and slapped a copy of his book down on the counter. Here, he said, this is for you. That man, concluded Villasenor, saved my life. He literally saved my life.

I got to thinking about that story again recently, wondering what books I'd read that had—if not saved—at least changed my life, and, as it happens, there were dozens. I credit books like *The Book of Tea, Zen Flesh, Zen Bones, Siddhartha* and the writings of Alan Watts with my early interest in Asia. It is because of those books that I majored in Asian history in college and ended up in Japan for an unforgettable year with Lilla and the kids. Novels like *The Stranger* and *The Plague* and plays like *Waiting for Godot* informed my general sense of being an outsider, while *The Sun Also Rises* stands out for me somehow as a window into that lost dreamy artistic life that one could lead as an expat. Stories by Isaac Bashevis Singer and Isaac Babel rekindled an interest in Judaism.

These are just a small handful of older books, and I won't go into all the new books that are still orbiting around in my brain. The larger point is that we need to remember the tremendous power of books to change our lives in ways we can't even imagine. People who don't read (and I've heard there are a few) are not nearly so available to change and grow. It is a form of mental arthritis they suffer from; they know exactly what they think and that's that. How sad. How tragic. How much more glorious it is to wake up each day to a brand new world, to doubt, to question, to reexamine all those platitudes we were so sure of when we were, say, twenty-five years old. I don't know about you, but I remember being twenty-five. How sure I was that a) God didn't exist, b) capitalism was doomed, and c) without a college education, you had zero future.

"Anyone who reaches the age of twenty-one and is not yet a communist is an idiot," my father used to say. "And anyone who is still a communist by the time he's thirty is also an idiot." You live. You learn. And the best journeys in life are fueled by books.

The Next Famous Person
March 2005

I'm right in the middle of a fabulous new novel, but you can't get your hands on it—at least not until it comes out sometime in May. This may sound unfair, but it's really just how the trickle-down world of books works. Publishers send booksellers samples of soon-to-be-released titles in hopes that we will get excited and order whole forests of them for the store. This novel I'm reading, *The History of Love* by Nicole Krauss, is, in my estimation, worth a tall stand of trees. Krauss is what used to be called a writer's writer, meaning she puts together heartbreakingly beautiful sentences, sentences that make you stop to read them again and again, they contain such wisdom and insight. What really does it for me, however, are her characters. They are bold and irrational and imperfect and full of raw emotions. You feel you know these people deep down in your bones; they are as familiar as your father's old overcoat.

Nicole Krauss is the kind of new fiction writer we are particularly drawn to, the kind we try our best to bring to Readers'. The problem is, of course, she is, as yet, unknown. But think about it: Isabel Allende, Anne Lamott, Michael Chabon, and every other writer we've brought to the store was once unknown, anonymous, a—you will forgive the expression—nobody. By my calculations, in the thirteen years of our existence, we've lured over a thousand writers to the store—many of them first-time authors. A thousand writers. That's not a bad batting average. And when they come to Sonoma, we can usually, depending on the day and the weather, generate a decent group to hear them read.

Now, naturally, we'd like to do better. And I think we could, if people only realized what they were missing. Imagine, for example, that you could go back in time. It's the early sixties and you're wandering around Greenwich Village when someone comes up to you and suggests you drop into this certain coffee house down the street tonight because a skinny kid from Minnesota named Bob Zimmerman is going to play some original folk tunes on his guitar. Or you're in City Lights Books in San Francisco and it's 1950-something and a poster says Jack Kerouac will be reading from his novel *On the Road*. Or you're in Paris in the 1930's and there's going to be a cozy book signing party for some guy named Henry Miller. You get the picture. Knowing what you know now, would you really pass up the opportunity to meet Bob Dylan or Jack Kerouac or Henry

Miller? Doubtful. Not that every poet or novelist who comes to Readers' Books is destined for that kind of stardom, but clearly some are. And what they have to say matters.

One autumn night in 1967, when I was a sophomore in college, I went to a poetry reading by Gary Snyder. He wasn't a new poet, but he was new to me, and he was just beginning to write what would become the major opus of his life. He read for two solid hours and what I remembered most is that I couldn't take my eyes off him. He was glowing, it seemed, and me—I was smitten. I was in love. The kind of love that ties you all up in knots and you don't care, it's so exhilarating. To this day, Gary Snyder remains one of my heroes. His voice still resonates in my heart.

I guess the point I'm trying to make is simple: up close, personal readings by new authors can alter the orbit of your life. They can change forever what you thought you once knew. They can make you think twice about your everyday existence, and, if you're lucky, a chapter or sentence or even just a casual phrase from their lips can send you scurrying down another rabbit hole altogether, where a different world awaits. This, to my way of thinking, is a good thing. This is why we need fiction: to get to the hard truth of who we are.

Oh, and by the way, Nicole Krauss will be appearing at Readers' Books on June 10th.

Creation
September 20, 2014

Some of you have wondered aloud as to how I go about writing these little ditties. What sort of excruciating medieval pain and torment do I endure to come forth with all these pearls of wisdom? Or, if there is no pain and torment involved, why then is it so bloody easy? What do I know about the creative process that the rest of you don't?

First of all, let me just confess that I don't think of what I do as creative. I've done "creative"—whole cloth, made up stuff—and in my experience that's hard work. Why? Because when you're writing fiction, you're always trying to cover your tracks. You want your character to be plausible and realistic, so what do you do? An example: You hand him an old C-melody saxophone and dress him in the most beautiful blue-striped double breasted suit and painted silk tie. You give him a slight, tell-tale limp left over from his traffic accident on Sunset Boulevard and a tiny scar on his forehead from where he hit the pavement. You let him stare too long into space. Then, as finishing touch, you put only the few snarky words he would ever say in his mouth.

I don't do any of that. No, I just sit down in front of a blank screen, and sooner or later I think of a sentence that sounds like me and I put it down. Then usually another sentence happens along that sort of goes with the first one, and so on and so forth, until to my amazement, I've strung together a whole page. Unless I am obsessing about a news item I just read, I honestly don't have a clue as to what I'm going to write in the beginning; it's entirely by the seat of my pants, which is more or less how I've led my life, so I guess you could say it's all of a piece.

I don't mean to suggest that I have nothing to say. I do. I just don't know what it'll be. This is a bit worrisome, because I've written so many essays now, and said so many things, that I often wonder whether something I wrote one day directly contradicts something I wrote the week before. I'm already sure that I'm starting to repeat myself, which means I'm running out of family anecdotes and such. Is this old age waiting in the wings? When you run out of stories? When it's all too familiar?

My main concern is coherence. I have too many relatives and a growing body of friends who, with each passing day, seem less and less coherent. They can't remember why they walked into a room. They can't remember the lyrics to their favorite song. Here in the bookstore almost everyone gets the title or the author or the color of the book they want wrong (I think I wrote a piece on that before). The truth is, things fall apart, and my main goal (sometimes it seems like my only goal) is to prevent that for as long as possible.

We eat right, therefore. We exercise. And when I sit down to put forth another one of these opuses, I always do my best. But please, don't ask me how I do it.

Here We Go Again
September 2003

In the Jewish calendar, the period spanning September and October represents an important time of return and renewal. There's a new year in the offing; time to hang up your flipflops and get serious again. When you step outside now, you feel that sly chill starting to creep into the air and, in the attic of your mind, you're already counting the days until the first snowfall. Not in California, of course, but I'm speaking paleolithically—i.e, when we used to count the days, back when we all wore bearskins and huddled around the fire.

Booksellers are perhaps not as far removed from the rhythms of the cave as some other professions. At the first hint of fall (and even before), we are all scurrying about like happy little Neanderthals, schlepping books hither and yon, bonding with our local postal clerks and UPS carriers, dusting the shelves, making ready. What are we up to? Why, returns!

Returns are the dark underbelly of bookselling. They signify the failure of all those fantastic titles we bought in the spring, the downfall of all those budding writers scribbling away in their rooms for years for a shot at stardom, all those books and people who "coulda been a contender." Not everyone can be a contender, of course; some must be also-rans. But if you care about the sanctity of the written word and the process of creativity, it still hurts to have to send your picks back to the publisher, where (like some horrible literary James Bond knock-off) they are all thrown together willy nilly and crushed into pulp. Some books, though, if I may be so bold, deserve their fate. Ta-ta Jay Leno; goodbye Rush Limbaugh, adios Howard Stern...

I should perhaps tell you that this was not always the case. In the old days (before the Great Depression), booksellers pretty much bought what they bought and kept what they couldn't sell, or marked down what they couldn't sell until someone couldn't resist it. This worked okay, but when the Depression hit, booksellers were loathe to take a chance on new, untested writers for fear of going out of business (which they did a lot of anyway), so a deal was struck with publishers. Now, when we buy new titles, the publishers expect a certain number will eventually come back unsold. It's part of the ebb and flow.

At Readers' Books, we try to be fair about returns. We are reluctant to return local authors, reluctant to return classics, reluctant to return books we've personally fallen in love with. Generally we give a book around six months to prove its mettle. After that, as a fellow bookseller once told me, "you'd better have a darn good reason to keep it."

At this time of year, however, as we prepare for the onslaught of new fall titles and the reprints of holiday favorites, I sometimes get this little pang. When I look around, our shelves seem almost bare and expectant. It's that time again. And I know it's going to start snowing any day now. I can feel it in my bones.

Where We Go Wrong
January 2006

Yesterday there was frost on our roof and a chill in the morning air as I started a fire in our woodstove. To do this meant balling up several sheets of newspaper with the kindling. Some of the news stories I crunched into the fire were forgettable, but there were others—stories about Iraq and Katrina and domestic spying and people trying desperately to get into this country to do jobs nobody here wants to do. And it made me think about America and memory and how rarely the two intersect.

These facts are crucial to me, because, as a bookseller, I am, as it were, all about memory. Who we are and where we came from—the long hard climb out of the primordial ooze, and what we learned along the way—is bookselling in a nutshell. Bookselling's also art and intellect and, well, civilized behavior.

America, perhaps because it so rich or so historically young and naïve, has never truly embraced her artists and intellectuals. We don't, to quote the current occupant of the White House, "do nuance." We tolerate artists and intellectuals, and, from time to time, we celebrate them by giving them medals of freedom and putting their faces on postage stamps, but what we really admire is how much they draw at the box office. A successful artist is one who can sell a novel for millions, or act in a movie for millions, or cut a record that goes platinum overnight. It's all about the money and it always has been. That's America.

Another observation: the adults around here who spend their days doing nuance are frequently trampled on or ignored by the infants who appear—at least at the moment—to run things.

When our son, Gideon, was just a wee thing, my wife got the idea for a movie. It would be a kind of parental remake of *King Kong* called "Baby." Kong, I mean Baby, was this ten-story tall enfant terrible toddling through a metropolis, gurgling and drooling while knocking over buildings and crushing steel bridges between his cuddly pink toes. He didn't destroy the city out of malice (he was just a baby after all); no, he did it whimsically, or as the result of his natural curiosity, or, at worst, as part of a tantrum, without regard to the consequences. How could you hate him for that? A little baby. (Okay, a big baby.)

As the fire started to catch in the woodstove, I tried to hold onto all these disparate thoughts. I am convinced that there are still plenty of good, rational adults out there who read, and remember, and wrestle with their doubts, and don't try to impose their faith on others—adults who can and will eventually correct the behavior of the infants among us. In this season, when memory itself seems to be going up the chimney in smoke, it is good to know we have each other to lean on.

What You Need to Know About Baseball
July 12, 2014

Although he never spent a moment of his life there, my dad was a devoted fan of the Cincinnati Reds. This was strange to me, because he came from New York, which was then the epicenter of the game. In fact, before he could even spell the word "Cincinnati," he used to hang around outside Yankee Stadium, where he'd wait hours sometimes just hoping to get a glimpse of Babe Ruth and Lou Gehrig.

After we moved to Southern California, I imagined that he would gravitate naturally to the Dodgers. That's where I ended up, drawn not so much by the team as by their colorful history and by the mellifluous voice of their announcer, Vin Scully. Scully knew everything there was to know about the game, but he was also a poet; he could describe in a few choice words the deep green expanse of Chavez Ravine's left field as well as the simple justice of an umpire's called strike three. For me, that was magic. That was romance. But whenever my dad and I spoke of baseball, the Reds were his team. In his youth, they were the habitual underdogs, he'd explain, always in the cellar, always underperforming. Of course, by the time I took any interest in the sport it was the seventies, and Cincinnati was a force to contend with. My dad couldn't be happier. Loyalty and patience (albeit from afar) had finally begun to pay off. Once in a while, when the Reds came to town, we would go to the game. We'd bet a nickel, him on the Reds, me on the Dodgers. And win or lose, a grand time would be had by all.

Last week my wife was away on a business trip. On the return leg, they routed her through Detroit, and I asked her to buy me a Tigers baseball cap, which is now sitting on my desk. It's a handsome thing, dark blue with an ornate white D in front. And I look pretty good in it, even though I've never actually been to Detroit, and I don't think I've ever seen the Tigers play in person. If you were to ask me why I need a cap from Detroit, the answer is, I don't (in fact, I don't actually need anything) but I want to support them. Not the team, mind you, but the town of Detroit. And not even the town of Detroit, but the idea of Detroit.

Detroit, as you probably know, is in terrible straits these days; people are leaving in droves, housing prices are in the single digits, unemployment is huge, the city has declared bankruptcy, and, just recently, about half the homes there had their water shut off for failure to pay the bill. There are whole blocks that have burned down and are being slowly turned back into farm land. The D on my cap could stand for "Detroit" or "down-and-out" or—I don't know—"done for." But I choose to let that D stand for "determined."

There are good, honest, hard-working people living there, after all, and even though their world has been shredded by what economists and academics call the "creative destruction" of capitalism, they are still there, still getting up every morning and putting cereal on the kitchen table, still shuffling one foot in front of the other, still trying to make ends meet. We in Sonoma may be a little better off than they are at the moment, but that could change in a heartbeat, you never know. And what doesn't change is the fact that they are our brothers and sisters. That's what this cap reminds me of. That's why I wear it. My dad, I think, would understand.

You Can't Go Home Again, So Don't Even Try
April 6, 2012

Every week it seems I get an email from an organization called Classmates. com. They want me me to pay them money for the privilege of reconnecting with my old high school chums. I think of it as kind of a dating service for people who live in the past. Whatever happened to old what's-her-name, you know, the one with the freckles and the padded bra that you were so enchanted by long ago? Apart from the fact that I can now barely remember who I went to high school with, there is a further dilemma: as a card-carrying member of the Baby Boom Generation, I have first-hand knowledge of how numerous (and thus anonymous) we were. Pasadena High School, my alma mater, was huge. Our graduating class alone had 1300 students. We couldn't all fit into the auditorium at once, and so our graduation—along with the other high school in town—took place in the Rose Bowl. My diploma had my name on it, I recall, but it could just as well have had a number.

Still, through the magic of the internet, there is now this company that wants me to bask in the good old days with Tom, Dick, and Harry. Which has a certain appeal, I admit, although I don't actually want to see these people again. I read the names of those alumni who have joined, and they look sort of familiar. I mean, once upon a time I must have seen them naked in gym and loaned them my notes from history and biology class, but that was 45-plus years ago.

The larger question is what is to be gained by going back to a small segment of life when our hormones were raging off the charts? High school was so fleeting, so indecipherable, after all: we were ugly, we were gorgeous; if someone looked at us cross-eyed, we'd be in despair and, in the next moment, we just knew beyond a shadow of a doubt that we would change the world.

A month or so ago, I thought about a skinny guy named Dan I'd roomed with briefly in college. He dropped out in his sophomore year to marry this knock-out French girl he'd met in Paris, and after that we lost touch with each other. He had an odd last name, and on a whim I typed it into Google. Bingo, a few keystrokes later there he was again, two generations removed, living now in a small town with his bride of long ago. He looked a bit like the zany old Dan I knew, but now he was a good deal wider around the middle, and time and gravity had taken hold with a terrible vengeance. The same applied to his once blonde and tres chic wife. They were standing proudly in front of a tract house in Georgia, a nice, gray-haired, very settled and very undistinguished couple gazing without fear or passion into the camera. They were not in despair, and, clearly, they had not gone on to change world. That is what I guess most of my classmates would look like if I ever saw them again. We try—each in our way—but in the end we mostly just put one foot in front of the other day after day, year after year. His phone number was there on the website, but after thinking it over, I decided not to call Dan out of the blue and disrupt his peaceful life. That would be so... high school.

A Number by Any Other Name
April 2012

I glanced at the calendar the other day, and between now and when the next newsletter appears in May it seems that I will, through the grinding of time, celebrate one more birthday. Not just another birthday, mind you, but my 65th birthday. On first blush, I cannot tell you how stunning this is, how absolutely shocking and ridiculous and inappropriate it feels, because the truth is, like my twin brother Jack Benny, I swear to you I have never (no really, Rochester, never) been older than 39.

65 has always been my father's age, and with good reason: By 65 you're supposed to have attained a certain gravitas. By 65, the kids have moved out, the house is paid for, the pets have stopped staining the carpet and mercifully expired. 65 means you've sold your business and travelled the world. In short, you've graduated to another realm, you've already done a great deal in life, perhaps everything you could ever imagine doing. This was true for my dad; for me, not so much.

Some things do apply, of course. For instance, around age 65, your vocabulary changes suddenly and without explanation. Now, when you see someone, the discussion often turns to grandchildren and their antics, or medications you're on and their unintended side-effects. You speak less and less about the new books you've read and more and more about the trouble you've had reading with your new bifocals. You now have friends who have actually retired, friends who have moved into gated communities or (gasp!) senior living facilities, and saddest of all, friends your age and younger who have died.

Which is why I continue to insist on being 39. Yes, my kids may have moved out of the house, but with the economy the way it is, you never know, they could come back. The house is no closer to being paid for, and, no matter what I say, my two ancient cats just shrug off the whole idea of death and go on about their business. And retirement? Retirement is so antiseptic and foreign-sounding. I mean, retire to what? I don't play golf. And there are only so many hours in the day that one can strum one's guitar, aren't there.

My father was retired when Lilla and I came back to California to start the bookstore. He was spending his days wasting away, mostly sprawled on the couch, watching baseball and CNN. He was not a happy man, but he cheered up right away when we put him back to work, and I firmly believe that we extended his life a good many years, just by giving him a reason to get up in the morning.

So please don't wish me a happy birthday when it happens. Or, if you must, just wish me a happy 39th. Because, honestly, that's how old I feel.

If You Want to Know Why this Night is Different from All Other Nights, I'll Tell You
March 23, 2013

At sundown, this coming Monday, Passover begins once again, as it has, for, lo, thousands of years. Jews all over the world will sit down together to eat and to remember how it felt to be liberated from Egyptian slavery. And even though this happened very long ago, we are nevertheless instructed to think of it as if it happened to us; we are supposed to somehow transcend time, embrace the freedom of our ancestors, and make it our own.

For me, Passover is akin to Thanksgiving: friends and family come together, there's lots of food (except for Yom Kippur, there's always food on Jewish holidays), everyone gets to hear what all the children and grandchildren are up to, old stories are retold for the umpteenth time, and the sentiment flows copiously. When I was growing up it was also an occasion for epic arguments about the nature of slavery in ancient times and how it related to oppressed people in modern times. Some folks add salt and pepper to their meal; we do that, too, but we often add a little argument as well to make it more interesting.

I recall one Passover in particular at my brother's house. Our old friend, Henry Sharp, was there, and, after we went over the part in the Seder where we talk about going forth from Egypt as if we were the ones being freed, Henry spoke quietly and with great eloquence. This Passover, he said, is special for me. Why? Because in 1945, on this exact date, I actually was set free from the concentration camp in Poland. So those words you just finished reading, they're not just words, they have a sweetness to them I understand and I remember very well.

There were tears in our eyes, and there were no arguments that evening. We ate and talked and sang the old songs we always sang. And afterwards, thanks to Henry, we all just basked in the glow of our newly realized freedom. It doesn't get any better than that.

Henry Sharp
August 13, 2011

Last Monday, after a long period of decline, our family's friend, Henry, died. On Tuesday, in accordance with Jewish tradition, we gathered together to help bury him. Each of us took turns shoveling some dirt over his casket, a practice which really focuses the mind.

Henry spent a few years of his youth in Auschwitz. His family was murdered there, but Henry somehow survived, and after the war he made his way to America. He fell in love with Rose, and together they ran a health food store here in Sonoma for many years. You may remember him.

At his funeral, people spoke about what a warm, generous person Henry was, which was true. Something they gave only glancing attention to, however, was his humor and zest for life. Henry loved Rose dearly, but they had both been through a lot, and, perhaps because they were both Jewish, they were not without strong opinions, which led inevitably to vituperative disagreements. My father told me that Henry, with a twinkle in his eye, sometimes referred to Rose—the love of his life—as the "War Department."

Henry and Rose were close to my parents. They went out together, celebrated Passover together, played Scrabble together, traded Yiddish jokes together. They were, all four of them, full of life, and inseparable. My parents are buried in the Beth Ami Cemetery in Santa Rosa. Very nearby is Rose's grave and now, right beside her, is Henry. They have their own special neighborhood, you could say. Rent free, green grass, plenty of time to argue the day away.

Everyone Talks About the Weather
February 23, 2013

Every morning this winter when I drive to work, I'm inevitably overcome with a deep, nearly religious sense of gratitude. Gratitude for the grass and for the sunlight glancing through the oak trees, gratitude for the vineyards that are suffused with that golden mustard between the rows, the rolling hills, the whole postcard of where we live. Most of all, I'll admit it, I'm very aware of and grateful for the unnatural warmth we're blessed with in February. I can say this without reservation because, you see, I once lived back East.

This morning I spoke to my wife by phone. She's currently in Massachusetts, where the temperature is hovering around 28 degrees and there's a good foot of snow on the ground. That's lovely, I suppose, in its own way, but you can't compare it with here, or rather, you can, but only at the risk of your marriage. No one back East wants to hear that there is an alternate universe where the sun is always (mostly) shining and people are always smiling at one another and jogging along in their shorts and the surf is always up. It makes them uncomfortable to know this, as though they are trapped, as though they've been doing something terribly wrong all their lives, something that can't ever be corrected. So I don't share much about the weather. My wife says it may snow again, that the sky is darkening up, and I nod sagely from 3,000 miles away and say, "Oh, really? I hadn't heard". I don't tell her what I'm wearing, which isn't much, or that I haven't used the heat in our house for days, or that the camellias are blooming outside our bedroom window. That would be mean, and that's not who I am.

Blasphemy
November 2004

For a long time now, I've been thinking a blasphemous thought, and that is that there are too many books in the world. Why blasphemous? Well, booksellers are prone to believe in the abundance of ideas. We've bought into the notion of progressive revelation—that life is a slow but sure hike up out of the slime and that books form the staircase. We think we need more books, not fewer. We know that if we just keep our eyes peeled, we'll discover the next Jack Kerouac thumbing a ride out on the highway, or the next Steinbeck, or the next Nabokov moldering away in his dowdy little college office somewhere in Vermont. With more books, in other words, we could be actual business contenders.

I still think that, but now after many years of shipping books in and then six months later shipping them back, I also know that for every ten books that are brought to the show, only maybe three are ever going to find a decent readership. The rest will end up, as they say, on the ash heap of history.

Three for ten is a bad percentage, of course, unless you are a baseball player. And as a bookseller, it means that more often than not, you spend your days toiling on behalf of UPS.

I had an employee who once offered a simple solution to this dilemma. He proposed that we stock no book that wasn't at least four hundred years old. That way we'd be sure to have a time-tested bestseller on our hands. You want romance? We've got *The Tale of Genji*. Adventure? Look no further than *Don Quixote*. Epic poetry? There's *The Iliad*, and of course, Homer's great sequel, *The Odyssey*. Science, you say? Take a gander at the latest triangles from Euclid. Humor? Aristophanes is a laugh riot, believe you me.

Now, naturally, in a bookstore such as this, we'd only have a couple dozen titles to think about, so we could dispense with the dreaded computer system altogether and get back to your basic pencil and yellow legal pad. There's a part of me (the Luddite part) that yearns for that, too.

Don't know what we'd do to spice up Christmas sales, but then maybe surrounded by such great ancient word masters, Christmas would revert to the more spiritual event it was originally intended to be. Say, what do you think of this? We could close for the last half of December. We could all stay at home and cuddle by the fire and bake cookies and cut out little old-fashioned wreaths and stuff like you see on Martha Stewart Living. We could...

Wait a minute. Close for December? Close for December?! Now that's blasphemy.

Paddling on Both Sides of the Canoe
November 2003

The other day we got an email from our old friend, Tony Miksak. Tony runs Gallery Books in Mendocino, a fine and venerable place not unlike Readers'— smack-dab in the middle of a tourist town, "user-friendly," "community oriented," "pro-children," etc. I put all these compliments in quotes for a reason, and that is because Tony recently had a difficult exchange with a group of his customers.

These folks wanted him to stop selling the writings of Bill O'Reilly, a neo-conservative voice of radio and TV. They didn't like him, thought he was evil. They so disliked him, in fact, that they wrote to Tony threatening that if he continued to sell O'Reilly's books, they would take their business elsewhere. (In Mendocino that means either a long drive or trading with Amazon.com—which also sells O'Reilly).

As it happens, Tony doesn't happen to much care for O'Reilly's point of view either, but in the interest of freedom of speech, he felt obliged to keep him on the shelf. After much discussion, he was unable to persuade these old lefties that tolerance and diversity lies at the heart of bookselling and that little is ever gained by "shooting the messenger."

Over the years, we have also had a few run-ins with customers who take it into their heads to become morality cops. Some examples:

º   An anonymous woman recently called to say that she would no longer shop at Readers' if David Ford, the author of two books promoting the benefits of marijuana, was allowed to speak at the store as scheduled in our newsletter. This woman contended that marijuana killed her daughter; by refusing to trade with us she imagined she would somehow strike a blow against the tragedy that had befallen her.

º   An anonymous man once called to tell us that he wouldn't shop here because we were having John Cornwell at the store. Cornwell is a devoted Catholic who wrote a book about how the intransigent policies of the Pope were slowly killing the Church, which troubled him greatly. It also troubled the man who called. He said it wasn't right to "criticize and tear down" the Church.

° Another anonymous woman called after Harry Wu came to speak at the Community Center. Wu was imprisoned in a Chinese labor camp for 17 years; he has been writing about Chinese injustice ever since, including how many products from China sold here are produced by slave labor. The woman had a lot to say about Mr. Wu. She said that the merchants of San Francisco's Chinatown wonder where he gets the money to travel about. She said that they think Harry Wu is a "front for the CIA." Unspoken here, of course, is the fact that the merchants of Chinatown derive their living from some of those products Wu claims are tainted by slave labor. But that's another story.

Everybody is entitled to an opinion, and by choosing where you spend or don't spend your money, you make a statement. There is a greater good, however, it seems to me, and that is the public's right to information. It may be that in these times neither the left nor the right can be relied on to offer new ideas or simply defend the truth. It may be that everyone is just too entrenched or too polarized or too scared.

I just want to say for the record that I can live with that. I am not afraid. I have learned to paddle on both sides of the canoe and still keep it right in the middle.

A man (unidentified) came in the store last week and asked for a book called *Shut up and Sing*. "It's a conservative book," he sneered. "You probably don't carry those in here."

"Oh, sure we do," I said. "We carry *Mein Kampf*. Big conservative seller."

The man looked at me blankly.

"It's a joke," I said.

He didn't get it.

Soul Customer
March 2010

Some people think we're all about retail at Readers' Books. Buying. Selling. Shipping. Receiving. Ka-ching, ka-ching, day in and day out. Well, I'm here to tell you that this is not true. Actually, when you drill down, as they say in Texas, retail is probably about the smallest part of our daily routine. No, mostly what we do around here is therapy.

I have an elderly customer—let's call her Anastasia—who phones at least six times a day with questions. Sometimes she wants to order books (she orders lots of books), but more often than not she wants to chat. She has—how shall I put this delicately—a religious bent. She claims, for example, that she is in direct contact with God, who has informed her in no uncertain terms that we are entering the end of days. Moreover, Anastasia has made it her mission to get me on board when the angels come down to evacuate the good folks from this wicked, wicked planet. At least, I think that's her mission.

She also wants me to spread various messages to the world—in particular, I should get word out to the Israeli government, tell them what's going on.

"But I don't know anyone in the Israeli government," I say.

"What are you talking about?" she yells. "This is heavy duty!"

What am I talking about. I don't honestly know how to answer this question—a) because it's not a question and b) because what I'm talking about is something called reality, which is far, far away from where Anastasia resides.

"You don't want to be left behind, do you?" she asks at least once a day.

"Oh, I dunno," I say. "I kind of like it down here. There's sunshine, guacamole. Why don't you go on without me, and just, you know, drop me a postcard when you get settled in heaven."

She is not amused.

Sometimes Anastasia yells biblical things at me, quotes and such. Sometimes she says that since I'm Jewish, I surely must know what various words mean in Hebrew and Aramaic and that I must be aware of the significance of certain evil numbers. (The fact, for instance, that Bantam Books is supposedly located at 666 Park Place in New York sends her into apoplexy.) But, of course, everything in Anastasia's imagination is connected and filled with portents. God doesn't shoot dice, she might say if she read Einstein.

Sometimes Anastasia sings to me over the telephone—she has a lovely voice— songs she composed herself about Jesus and lambs and God's glory and Jerusalem. Sometimes she says I should record her songs and send them to the Israeli government.

"What would they do with them?" I ask.

"What do you mean?" she says, outraged. "These are the words of the Lord."

I have tried to limit the amount of time I spend with Anastasia each day. I have tried to keep our conversations strictly to books—which ones she wants to order, which ones are out of print, which ones are filled with right wing messianic venom that attacks blacks and Jews and Catholics and gays. Lord knows, I have.

Don't get me wrong, I like Anastasia. She's a first-rate character, and, when I get to be her age, I only hope I'll have the same passion for comparative literature as she does for the Second Coming. Right now, though, whenever the phone rings and I hear her voice on the other end, I sometimes wish I had listened more closely to my parents back when they said that maybe I should think about med school.

Clothes Make the Man
May 2005

Lately, I've taken to wearing ties to work. Sometimes just a tie. Sometimes a tie and a sports jacket. Not every day, but maybe three days a week, which, since I figure I work nine days a week, equals about a third of my total time at the bookstore. I didn't think it would be any big deal, but I have to say that I am astounded at people's reactions. Comments range from: "How was your day in court?" to "Going to a bar mitzvah?" to "So, who died?"

At first, I tried to play along with the humor. I said I was going to a job interview at Walmart. I said I had an unexpected appointment with the IRS. I said nobody I knew died, but I was still hopeful. Stuff like that. Then, after a while, I realized that I had genuinely upset some folks by daring to show up in a tie. They didn't like it at all. One of my pals at the post office told me that I'd turned up three times that week in a tie and that he hadn't worn a tie more than three times in his entire life. I said, "That's nothing to be proud of." And he protested that he was proud of it. This got me to thinking about things like conformity and dress codes and authority symbols, topics I visited again and again growing up in the 50's and 60's. It's hard to imagine that any adult is still stamping his feet and raging about these things any longer, but you never know. My wife tells me she wonders about grown men walking around in baseball caps and sneakers, thinks it is generally a demeaning, stupid look.

Of course, the real reason I started wearing a tie has nothing to do with that. It's about professionalism. Lawyers wear ties, as do doctors and bankers and accountants and basketball coaches. Even my brother the pharmacist puts on a tie at work. Teachers used to wear them regularly when I was a lad. (I'm told they don't so much anymore.) But all these persons are "professionals." As am I. Bookselling is a distinguished profession, and shouldn't I therefore honor it in some distinguishing way?

To be fair, not everyone is appalled or threatened by the sight a man in a tie. Women, once they get over their shock of a "dressed up" person in a small town, seem to heartily approve. And women are most of my customers, so I am not too worried.

Many years ago I wrote a short story called "Clothes Make the Man." It was about an ordinary Joe who, suddenly homeless, and down to his last little bundle of cash on earth, decides to kill himself. But before he does, he wanders into Brooks Brothers where he blows everything on a stylish look. Of course, the moment he walks out the door, his life changes for the better. Going up the elevator in the building he plans to dive off, he meets Moira, a young, beautiful girl. There is mutual attraction by the time they reach the 12th floor. Death, he decides, can wait a bit. She invites him to coffee to meet her Uncle Harold who owns the hotel. Harold, who is childless and looking for an heir, sees potential in this young man who clearly adores his niece and ends up offering him a job. In the course of the afternoon (and with the help of a few new fashionable rags), the world has become his oyster. That's the gist of the story. I'm not suggesting anything like that will happen to me, but I do believe that impressions count for something in this world, and in business, like everything else, it's always prudent to put one's best foot forward.

Now, when people ask me where I am going with that tie on, I look them in the eye and give it to them straight: to work, I say.

In My Father's House are Many Chicken Coops
March 2009

My father had many careers. When he turned sixty he went back to night school and became a lawyer. It was a Talmudic quest on his part; he loved going to school and he pictured himself in court someday splitting hairs with brilliant minds, justice versus mercy, all that. Of course attending law school is a far cry from practicing law, and when he learned what lawyers actually do to rake in the bucks, he quit in disgust. But before he was a lawyer, he was a pharmacist. And before he was a pharmacist he was, for a brief time, a chicken farmer.

You might wonder what a nice Jewish boy who grew up among the bright lights and skyscrapers of Manhattan would see in tending chickens, but, in fact, it was a natural path. In the thirties, while trying to eke out a living through the Great Depression, my dad became smitten with political idealism. Roosevelt and Karl Marx were like family in his living room. He also was deeply interested in Zionism. Zionism then was not fraught with all the baggage the New Left has given it today. In those days, Jews were the downtrodden, the underdogs, and the notion that they could part with their centuries-old urban habits and reclaim their ancestral homeland was—pardon the pun—groundbreaking.

Many young American Jews were given instruction in farming to prepare them, ostensibly, for service in the eventual Jewish state. My Uncle Irving worked on one such establishment in New Jersey. Nowadays I suppose the chicken farm where he spent the summer of 1936 might be called a terrorist training camp, depending on which side of the historical fence you are on. At any rate, chickens were not simply chickens to my father; they were an ideal, the culmination of man's honest sweat and toil, socialist realism personified.

World War II interrupted this dream of his and, by the time he was home from the Army, he had a family and Israel was already a nation. In 1952, however, he tried once more to work out his chicken karma. He rented two large coops in Hempstead, Long Island, then a wilderness of truck farms and open expanse. Several hundred chickens lived in one of them and we—my father, mother, brother and I—lived, tar-papered, inside the other. We lasted perhaps one year in this wretched condition. My memories of that time are vague. I was only five. I do remember being always cold and eating way too many eggs.

Sneeze and the World Sneezes with You...
July 19, 2015

One of the arguments made in favor of moving to Los Angeles had nothing whatsoever to do with the fantastic new job my wife was getting or the cultural diversity or the great food or reconnecting with old friends. I mean, those are all splendid reasons to go anywhere. I could make those very same arguments and hop on the next plane to Tokyo. Well, my wife probably wouldn't have scored that great job in Tokyo, but if she did, boy, who knows what could happen?

No, the argument I never mentioned openly was that moving to LA would signal an end to the allergies that have plagued me every spring in Sonoma. Silly me—I thought that coming here to this place, which is mostly paved over and polluted and riddled with drought, a place that has fewer and fewer plants and trees, a place where everyone is volunteering to let their lawns return to dust, would somehow let me breathe again.

Of course, it sounds idiotic on its surface—breathe in LA? But for at least four months out of each year I could barely breathe in Sonoma. I tried to come to terms with it, naturally: I took various drugs and tried all sorts of homeopathic this and that. Nothing worked for long.

I even briefly tried to embrace my malady and turn it into something nourishing for the whole town. We created a Vintage Festival after all, and Napa does something around mustard. I ran the thought by certain now retired members of the City Council. How about an Allergy Festival in May? People could build floats just like they do for the Rose Parade in Pasadena, only these floats would be sponsored by CVS or Walgreens or the companies that make Allerest and Xertec and Kleenex. They could be elaborate and inventive and cost hundreds of thousands of dollars to build. Our young people would have gainful employment at last. Tourists would flock here from far and wide. (Oh, wait. They already do that). And there could be sneezing and wheezing contests around the Plaza, and punk bands with names like Insomnia and Phlegm to entertain the choked up crowds.

Needless to say, the local politicians I spoke with looked askance at this notion, and like so many ideas that are ahead of their time, it went nowhere.

Now that I'm here, I would like to say that moving to LA helped. But the truth is, there are other allergies in this neck of the woods, not the same as in Sonoma perhaps, but just as threatening to my delicate sinus passages. So I was wrong. And unfortunately, I have a year-long lease, so I can't simply turn around and move back, even if there was no cultural diversity or great food to be had.

The Foreigner Comes Home
September 22, 2012

It was my great good fortune to see *The Foreigner* at the Sonoma Community Center this week, a charming, laugh riot of a play, well-acted, with an amazing cast and a plot that pulled at all my heart strings.

It reminded me of a drama teacher I had back in high school, a man who, even though he has long since passed away, seems to be playing a larger and larger role in my life. His name was Abel Franco. He was one of the most beloved teachers at Pasadena High, and I took his drama class three years in a row. I wasn't much of an actor, in fact, my aspirations didn't extend much beyond seeking to be an extra in all the many productions we put on. I was listed as Servant with Fruit Platter in *Taming of the Shrew*, for example. Now you might not think you could do much with a part like that, but I managed to accidentally dislodge one of the plastic oranges on my platter as I crossed the stage and watched nonplussed as it bounced into the audience to gales of laughter. It was one of those moments all actors remember, even non-actors like me.

But Mr. Franco's class was about so much more than acting. He introduced me to haiku and Jack Kerouac and great books on Zen—*The Book of Tea* and *Zen Flesh, Zen Bones*. We did scenes from Eugene Ionesco's *Rhinoceros* and *The Chairs*. We did Albee's *The Sandbox* and *Who's Afraid of Virginia Woolf?* and of course Beckett's *Waiting for Godot*. This was all dazzling new terrain to me and I could not stop myself from exploring it .

Mr. Franco also used his own life's path as an example of how the arts can make us human. He'd been a G.I. during World War II, a rifleman plodding his way up the boot of Italy. One day I remember him telling us how, towards the end of the war, the Germans were running out of recruits and they were reduced to taking fourteen and fifteen year old kids, putting uniforms on them, handing them rifles, and sending them to the front. They surrendered in droves, he said, but not all of them. What did you do? we asked. That was when we learned the truth: that Mr. Franco's job was to shoot the ones who stood their ground. It was war, after all. What choice did he have. At first, I was stunned when he said this. And yet, twenty years later, here he was in Southern California. And what was he doing? Teaching fourteen and fifteen year old kids like me, trying (perhaps subconsciously) to atone for that sad time, with art and compassion.

And whenever I see a play that makes me smile or laugh or cry or nod with understanding, I think about that teacher who meant so much to me. At times we may all be prisoners of our circumstance, but there are almost always opportunities in our lives to do the right thing and step beyond them. For that I will always be grateful.

On Giving and Taking
March 30, 2013

I've been thinking about tips and discounts lately, and what they might say about us as a society. Every Tuesday, it seems, I find myself at the checkout counter in Sonoma Market, and when my few pitiful purchases make their way to the man or woman standing at the cash register, I am impelled to say something like, "It's Tuesday, and I am an elderly person." They have yet to quibble with me about this, so I assume they agree and, then, almost magically, my bill is reduced by 10%. The truth is I don't really need a discount on Tuesday, but I can justify it any number of ways. Maybe they're doing this out of respect for the elderly, or maybe there are a disproportionate number of older folks who are living close to the edge, and this is Sonoma Market's way of dishing out a little justice, or maybe it's not about justice at all. Maybe they're just looking to increase customer loyalty and market share, and old people have to eat, don't they?

The same vague arguments can be applied to tipping in this culture. We typically tip waiters and waitresses and shoe shiners, limo drivers and hair-dressers, although the latter sometimes make a fair amount of money. When we lived in Japan, it was considered rude to tip a waiter or a cab driver; what they charged was what they got and to be given more implied—I don't know—that you thought they were doing more than their level best and deserved extra credit, even though in their mind they were always doing their level best. It was, in short, an insult to the way they lived.

I'm not suggesting discounts and tips are "wrong," but I've never been able to figure out the rationale. We don't have a tip jar at Readers' Books, even though everyone here works like dogs for little money and offers (I think) a real and valuable service, pointing folks to just the right book. And we tried, you may remember, offering discounts through our Readers' Regulars cards, those yellow things some people still wax nostalgically over, but that was costing us thousands of dollars each year and when the recession kicked in that was one of the very first things we had to jettison.

I have a cousin who is a lawyer, and he spends his day billing folks almost every time he opens his mouth. It's $300 an hour or, if he only talks for six minutes or less, it's $30. I'm sure his advice is valuable, but does it compare with me telling someone why they should read the new Kent Haruf novel, *Benediction*, or Marisa Silver's splendid book, *Mary Coin*? Why do we often toss a dollar or two into a street musician's guitar case and, a minute later, pass by a homeless beggar with our hands firmly in our pockets? Somebody tell me, please. I'd really like to know.

The Check's in the Mail
June 7, 2014

Among the many strange items popping up in the news these days is the following: certain "family" oriented organizations are now in an uproar over the latest stamp put out by the United States Postal Service because it features the smiling face of Harvey Milk, the gay political activist from San Francisco whose life was cut short by another San Francisco politician who not only owned a gun, but who, unfortunately, had some serious anger management issues.

That Harvey Milk was literally the face of the gay rights movement in this country, just as Cesar Chavez and Rosa Parks and others were similarly the faces of their respective movements, does not seem to matter to these old-fashioned family folks. They don't seem to recognize the fact that times have changed, and that people today are generally more of the "live and let live" persuasion. Some examples: We're not (most of us, at least) looking under our beds for communists anymore; we're not digging fallout shelters; we're not lynching black men for chatting with our sisters; we're not beating up black children who dare to attend our schools; we're not (except in a few outlying places like Texas and Oklahoma) locking up our kids for life because they smoke dope and like rock'n'roll. Women may now be seen walking down the street in what would have been called a bra years ago. And (worse, or better) many women don't even bother wearing bras anymore. People still get married, of course, but if their primary interest is in having a family, guess what, a marriage license is no longer required. Ditto for the blood test. Oh, so many things have changed.

Still, there's this clinging, rear-guard action. They don't like Harvey Milk. Or what he stands for. They don't want to see his face on a postage stamp. They're asking people to boycott the stamp, and, if someone sends you a letter with a Harvey Milk stamp on it (heaven forfend!), they're suggesting you mark it "return to sender." Then somehow all this sinful and satanic stuff will all go away.

My reaction, as you may imagine, is slightly different. I never knew Harvey Milk personally. What I learned about him came from reading the newspaper or watching events on television, but it was always clear to me that whatever one thought about gays and their lifestyle, here was someone who was not only articulate, but absolutely unafraid to be himself. And that kind of courage turned out to be contagious.

When you take a step back from this, it seems so silly and childish to get into a snit over a postage stamp, although, of course, there are stamps I also find distasteful. I'm not crazy about Charlton Heston, for instance (all that prattle about prying his rifle out of his cold, dead hands), and I can't ever recall buying any Ronald Reagan stamps, either. But if someone were kind enough say, to send me a check with a Ronald Reagan stamp on it, hey, I'm good.

So here's the plan: I'm buying a whole slug of Harvey Milk stamps, and at the end of the month I'll use them to mail out payments to all my vendors. Some of them are sure to be "family" oriented firms. Some of them, I know, have strong opinions about homosexuals. Maybe when they see his face on the envelope, they'll cringe and send it back unopened. God, I hope so. As Harvey himself might say, that would show how beautiful capitalism really is.

A Sad Way to End the Year
January 2016

I could not let it slip that our dear friend, Kathy Gerletti, the vivacious redhead at the Bay Street post office, died suddenly over the holidays. She was only in her fifties, and the details are vague, but I saw her before Christmas and she seemed fine. Then, when I returned to Sonoma in January, she was no more.

Even though it was small and cramped and a little bit out of our way, we always made a point of bringing our packages to the Bay Street office. We did so in part because the post office officials were regularly threatening to shut it down, but mostly we brought our business there because of Kathy. She was an amazing people person—not just energetic, but upbeat, and generous to a fault.

People invariably shake their heads and say it's a tragedy whenever someone dies before their time, but tragedy is an overused term, in my opinion, and this was more than that. This was robbery. Kathy was stolen away from us and God only knows why.

I know all the postal staff around Sonoma is grieving her loss, but there has been very little mention of it, except for one sweet letter to the Index Tribune. Kathy was a real gem in our town, and our world is a poorer place without her bright smile and relentless good cheer.

And now, every time I walk into a post office, I know for a fact that I'll be thinking about her. I'll be glancing all around and I'll be hoping that somehow she'll be there again, talking to customers, counting out the stamps, doing three things at once even while she hums to herself behind the counter. This is magical thinking, granted. And you know what? I don't care. Kathy was just that kind of person. She was alive; she was magical.

Why Poetry Still Matters (to Me)
March 31, 2012

The gods have designated April as Poetry Month, and one never wants to look askance at the gods, does one? Actually, I have to confess that I began my literary life as a poet. In high school, when I fell under the spell of e.e. cummings and Rimbaud, I dashed off all manner of lovely if inconsequential drivel, which my teachers praised, and which was subsequently published in the high school literary magazine. This, of course, led to a swelling of my ego, which caused me to enroll at the University of New Mexico in order to study with the poet Robert Creeley. I was going places, you see, although my father was not so taken with this idea. A child of the Great Depression, he wanted me to be a lawyer or a pharmacist or—dare he even say it aloud—a doctor, something that would always assure me a decent paycheck and a roof over my head. I wanted instead to be a poet, which to him was like me saying I wanted to be a butterfly. Still, good parent that he was, how could he deny my improbable dream?

Midway through my junior year, things tilted in the universe and I called my father up. Dad, I said, I've had an epiphany. I realize now that you were right. I'm never going to earn a living as a poet, and now I want to do something different, something more commercial. Great! he said. Terrific! What do you want to do? I want to write novels, I said earnestly.

There was a long silence over the phone. I could almost see his eyes rolling and his brain whirring: Oh, Lord, here we go again.

Now, many careers and many years later, my late father and I have come at last to an understanding. Now I get to host poets at the store, I get to read their work and sell their books and rejoice at their heart-felt wisdom. And while I still don't have a decent paycheck to rely on, I do at least have a roof over my head. My dad would have liked that. Although he would probably think of it as poetic justice.

Summer Musings
July 2004

The other day, I was filing a resume from one of our thousands of typically overqualified, cheerful, and eager job applicants when I came upon a startling discovery. On our application form, under the Former Employment section, was one of those fill-in-the-blank statements that read: "reason for leaving." At least that's what it should have read. Instead it was: "reason for living." A mistake, obviously, and granted, most people had politely ignored it and penned in their assorted reasons for "leaving"—e.g., switched schools, company went bankrupt, got married. Others crossed out "living" and wrote in "leaving" before responding. And a very few people had attempted to answer the question at hand. Reason for living? "To shake hands with eternity." "To merge with the Great Oneness." "I hope someday to diffuse the planet with light."

It struck me that asking prospective employees what possible reason they had for living might not be such a bad thing. After all, nobody asks you that anymore. All week long we just get up, put our clothes on, eat our Cheerios, and go merrily or reluctantly or unconsciously off to work or school or whatever without thinking about the underlying implications. Just posing the question would be useful, I believe. And it can't be verboten to wonder about that on a job application, can it? I mean, it's personal, but it's not like asking nosy questions about your weight or age or sexual preferences. A person who has a decent reason for living, arguably, would be a valuable asset to any company.

Up until now, we've always skirted the "reason for living" issue by asking trick questions, such as—if stranded on a desert island what five books would you choose to take with you? Of course the real response to this is "Don't be an idiot. If stranded on a desert island I would have had no chance at all to choose my reading material." But the question has merit because if someone answers say, "any five books by Danielle Steel," well, it gives you a clue as to their reading habits.

We have another open-ended question as well: "What assets would you bring to Readers' Books?" Again, there are no wrong answers, but if all the applicant says is "I love books," or "I love to read," I must confess, it is troubling. The book business, I explain to them, has something to do with reading, but that's only the tip of the iceberg, or at least the first step in a long arduous trek. It's a bit like equating getting kissed with having a baby. You need to be able to do it and enjoy it, but the real journey is much more involved.

But let me put it to you another way. If you are lucky or clever enough to land a job here at Readers' Books, you'll have to have a reason for living. Which, in the end, is probably worth more than the job itself.

What Goes Around Needs, Eventually, to Come Around
March 21, 2015

Every now and then, the vacuum cleaner here at Readers' Books breaks down. We use it virtually every morning, so this is not what you'd call a surprise. And when it finally gets so bad that it is beyond our limited technical capacity to fix, I throw it in the back of my car and drive it to Azef, the old Iranian gentleman in Santa Rosa who takes care of such things. Azef, I imagine, came here a long time ago, though he still speaks with a heavy accent. We don't talk politics when I come in, mostly what we talk about is retail—how it's changed over the years, how it's harder and harder for the little guy to get ahead. Sometimes we discuss the weather—how it's getting hotter and drier, which of course is eventually going to make it harder and harder as well. Azef has a long, sweet, suffering demeanor. And when you look at him you know that he is accustomed to things getting harder and harder.

I mention Azef as a way of thinking about Iran, and how bewildered we seem to be when the subject of Iran comes up. There are folks right now, important folks who occupy high positions in the United States government, who say the most outlandish things about Iran. Iran, they suggest, is the very nexus of evil. Iran is worse than ISIS. Iran is crazy. Iran can never be trusted. If Iran ever gets its hands on the atom bomb it will be the end of the world as we know it.

What is true about Iran is that it has had a long and checkered relationship with the West, and, because of that, many people in Iran have—at best—mixed feelings about America and Britain. There was that time, you may or may not remember, back in the 1950's, when our CIA engineered a coup to overthrow a duly elected Iranian government headed by a man, a socialist named Mossadegh, and replace him with their guy—the Shah, Reza Pahlevi. And then, of course, the Shah had the CIA train and equip his secret police, SAVAK, who kept the country in its brutal grip for decades. I am not making this up; this is the truth. It is available in history textbooks and old Time Magazine articles. You can even hear about it occasionally on other radio stations besides KPFA.

Eventually, they had a revolution in Tehran and the Shah was forced to flee. The revolution was not pretty. They rarely are. Nor was it pro-American either, which would hardly be surprising. The mullahs, the religious leaders, seized control. Their minions took our embassy staff as hostages and shouted "Death to America" in the streets. Many more secular Iranians who were fond of American music, American literature, and dress styles, found themselves suddenly out of favor and scared. Times got harder.

At this point maybe I ought to mention another thing we did which many Americans have conveniently forgotten but which riled the Iranians. We lent our support to Saddam Hussein during the Iran-Iraq War, one of the bloodiest conflicts ever in that region. Saddam was our guy back then. He was going to teach those Iranians a lesson. If you don't believe me, you can always check out the old news stories and photos of him smiling with American officials. The war, which ended in a stalemate more or less where it began (except for the fact that millions of young men and women were gassed and slaughtered), understandably left a bitter taste in the mouths of many Iranians.

Which brings me to the present day. The Iranians are pursuing nuclear energy, ostensibly for peaceful purposes. There is much we should be wary of here. There is, after all, a vast Sunni-Shia struggle going on, lots of moving parts, and perhaps it wouldn't be such a good idea to add nuclear weapons to the mix. On the other hand, the biggest terrorist threats Americans have faced have all come out of places like Saudi Arabia and Pakistan. They are supposedly our allies, although why we call them that is beyond me. We have almost nothing in common. Saudi Arabians help fund ISIS. In Saudi Arabia, people are publicly flogged for adultery, and women are arrested for trying to drive a car. Pakistan is run by its military and already has nuclear weapons. Pakistan is where we found Osama Bin Laden living. Oh, and did I mention there were no Iranian commandos on those planes that slammed into the World Trade Center?

Iran is a country with a long, proud, complex history. Like any country, it has all kinds of people, with all kinds of needs and vested interests. Many young Iranians, I'm sure, are interested and attracted to the United States. Others, with good reason, still fear us. In the last half century, Iran has endured many hard times; we should always bear that in mind. It may have a few flamboyant leaders (like its former president) who act and say ridiculous things that make Americans uncomfortable. To be fair, we've had more than our share of pompous, asinine politicians on this side of the pond, too. That doesn't make us a crazy, evil country. And if we are ever going to move forward, then the same standard should also apply to Iran.

What He Meant, I Guess
January 4, 2014

One of the last phrases my dad said to my mom before he drifted off forever in his hospital bed was "be brave." I've been pondering that for over ten years now. Did he really mean, be brave? Or just act brave? And is there a difference? Was "be brave" some kind of secret expression between them? He and she came out of a different era, of course, when times were tough and a big premium was placed on character and bravery and such. That's how they got through the Great Depression and World War II, by being brave. That's what we believe.

But what does that mean? I've concluded, after much thought, that being brave, or acting brave, which is just pretending to be brave, has a lot more to do with enduring. Bad things happen and you soldier on. And you do this not because of some mystical inner quality of strength you possess, not because you're an American and Americans are rugged individuals, but because, in the end, you have no choice. Oh, you could curl up and die, I suppose, and there are a few very frail souls who do that when they lose their dog or their spouse or the stock market plunges. Most of us though, thankfully, have enough moxie to still get up the next morning; we drink our coffee, glance at the newspaper, go about our lives. Are we hurt? You bet. Is there a hole left that will never be filled? Probably so. But we trudge on, and that's a blessing, not just for ourselves, but for civilization at large.

Whenever I consider bravery I am reminded of that glorious passage in *Catch-22*, where Captain Nately (I think that was his name), a 20-year old pilot, a kid from Yale, is sitting in a whore house in Rome, talking politics with a 107-year old Italian gentleman. The old guy says he is a very moral man, that when Mussolini came to power, he was all for him. Then, when Hitler's tanks rolled in, again, he raised his arm in salute. Now that the Americans have liberated us, he shouts, "Viva America!" Nately, the idealist, thinks this is appeasement, opportunism, or, at best, mealy-mouthed double talk. Don't you stand for something? Wouldn't you rather die on your feet, he asks, than live on your knees? The old man gently corrects him. No, no, he says, you live on your feet and die on your knees. And right after their chat, Nately strolls out the door and gets killed by a sniper.

Bravery is what gets you through to tomorrow. We can stand for all kinds of causes, but bad things happen all the time, and life, as any alcoholic can tell you, is a day-by-day event. In that sense, we are all brave, I suppose. Sometimes the best thing you can do for yourself is just keep your head down and dig a deeper foxhole.

Acknowledgements

Whenever I watch the Academy Awards, there's always this moment when the winner stands up there in the floodlights and says, in effect, I didn't do this alone. In Hollywood, that's especially true, because almost every film you see is the product of many individuals and lots of time and money and committees and yada yada yada. So yes, they have to reel off a long list of little people who are really responsible for their golden Oscar.

In the case of this book, my list is somewhat smaller, but, to my mind, no less important. I have to thank the good folks at Readers' Books for nudging and nursing this thing along—among them Jude Sales, my partner in crime and chief financial officer, Rosie Lee, compiler of essays and engineer of style, Thea Reynolds, Barbara Fetesoff, Barbara Hall, and Silver Hall (no relation to Barbara). I also should thank Gia Sorenson (nee Coturri) who used to work here and who graciously proofed the whole damn thing for coherency, typos, etc. Thanks to Leslie Carlson and Ron Raley, my old friends in Hollywood, who did the layout and brilliant graphic design. Many thanks to Chester Arnold for his contribution of the fabulous cover painting, which so aptly describes the title. I ought to also thank my wife, Lilla, for reading these things over in the original before they ever went to print (half the time before she'd even had her morning coffee), and, with her blue pencil, deleting most, if not all, of my callous remarks. It's only because of her that I sound like the civilized person I pretend to be. I should thank my parents, too. A lot of these tales revolve around their wisdom and antics, after all. And the older I get, the more my life seems to resemble theirs. Finally, I have to thank all the customers I've had the pleasure of knowing all these many years. Your constancy and passion for literature is what has kept this bookstore afloat through good times and bad.

These essays are pieces of my life, it's true. But they are also, I hope, pieces of yours as well. We are bound together, as it were, by this book, and by so much more. So, thanks.